DON'T KISS TOADS

Finding Your Prince or Princess

DON'T KISS TOADS

A Study of Dating for Christian Teens

SANDRA HUMPHREY

CHRISTIAN COMMUNICATIONS
P.O.BOX 150
NASHVILLE, TN 37202

Published by Christian Communications
A division of the Gospel Advocate Co.
P. O. Box 150, Nashville, TN 37202

ISBN 0-89225-334-7

CONTENTS

A Note to Teachers

In the famous fairy tale, the princess had to kiss a toad to find her charming prince. Luckily, better ways exist to find one's prince or princess!

"Who can I date?" "Where shall we go?" "Should we go steady?" "How do I feel about the 'Three D's'—dancing, drinking and drugs?" "Is this the one I should marry, and am I ready for marriage?"

These are tough decisions, and they have to be made at a relatively young age. A wise person can substitute knowledge for experience, though, and avoid making tragic mistakes. To help teens gain this crucial knowledge is the purpose of *Don't Kiss Toads*.

The Bible principles that apply to dating are often the same ones that affect other phases of Christian living. So not only does this study involve matters of keen interest to young people, but it will supply them with biblical principles essential to mature Christian living.

For class use, sharing and molding of attitudes through group discussion of the "To Think About" section at the end of each chapter should be the heart of each lesson. It is important, though, for students to look up the scripture references included with each chapter. Without this biblical basis, the class could become simply an exchange of opinions which, although interesting, would not contribute significantly to spiritual growth.

Consider reading each chapter's scriptures during class time to make sure the material is covered. This, together with good discussion, will probably require at least two weeks per lesson.

Marriage is probably the main outside factor that determines personal happiness and spiritual destiny. *Don't Kiss Toads* is aimed at helping Christian young people prepare for the happily-ever-after kind of marriage.

CHAPTER 1

For This Cause

"Let us hear the conclusion
of the whole matter: Fear
God, and keep His
commandments: for this is
the whole duty of man."
Ecclesiastes 12:13

"Should I wear the blue sweater or the yellow one?"
"Would it be better to take Physics or Chemistry?"
"Should I go on to college; and if so, which one?"

Life can be described as a series of decisions. Many are small, and some are big; but the three most important decisions you will ever have to make are these:

1. A decision concerning your relationship to God
2. Selection of a career
3. Choice of a person to marry

Each of these three tremendous decisions is usually made while those involved are relatively young. Because of this they have little actual experience on which to base their decisions, so it is necessary to substitute study and knowledge for experience to avoid making tragic mistakes. This series has been prepared to help you form some personal guidelines in at least one of these three crucial areas that of dating and marriage.

MY GOD AND I

Most of us would probably agree that the first major decision listed, one's relationship to God, is supposed to be the nucleus about which life revolves. Each person who has ever lived was created by God and will eventually return to Him for an accounting (2 Corinthians 5:10). It would be foolish not to agree, then, that the overriding factor in every decision should be to please God.

Yet this cannot be simply a mental agreement. One must act upon this realization in every phase of his life, particularly while he or she is young and laying the foundation for life (Ecclesiastes 12:1).

CHOOSING A CAREER

Your decision concerning a career is also obviously important. A person who is unhappy with his job finds it extremely difficult to be content or feel fulfilled. That is why it is really worth hanging on and getting the training necessary for a job you will really enjoy.

To a Christian, however, a job is simply an "avocation" or sideline. It is a necessary but not all-consuming means of providing for physical needs.

God gave the simple equation that he who would not work should not eat (2 Thessalonians 3:10). He also branded the person who will not provide for his own physical responsibilities "worse than an infidel" (1 Timothy 5:8).

But serving God is a Christian's true "vocation" (Ephesians 4:1). Acquiring material possessions is never a satisfying goal in life (Matthew 16:26), as seen by the unhappy lives of most millionaires.

THE PERSON YOU MARRY

Judged by its effect on your main goal of serving God, choosing the right career is much less important than choosing the right marriage partner. The person you marry will have an indelible effect on your life. He or she will be the greatest outside factor in determining your way of life and consequently your eternal destiny.

A happy marriage is one of the most satisfying pleasures on earth; an unhappy marriage is one of the most bitter. Yet despite the tremendous effect your marriage will have on your future, God has laid down this very stiff law:

> **A husband and wife are bound to each other until death.**
>
> *(Romans 7:2-3; 1 Corinthians 7:39)*

If only marriages were really "made in heaven," there would be no problem. But God only seals in heaven the marriages people arrange on earth. That is why it is so terribly important to make all the preparations possible to ensure success *before* you fall in love and marry!

WHAT DO YOU EXPECT OF MARRIAGE?

In Oriental societies of the past, young couples were matched and married without ever having met one another. And those marriages were usually happy and successful.

Even when divorce was allowed, the divorce rate from such marriages was always below that of countries where young people dated and selected their own mates. But this was because Oriental young people were brought up expecting such an arrangement to work.

We have been brought up very idealistically, however, wanting and expecting a great deal from marriage. The Oriental philosophy led them to view any *virtue* in their mate as an unexpected blessing. Married people today are more prone to concentrate on the *flaws* in their mate and view them as a disappointment and reason for divorce and a second try.

But in God's sight, a marriage contract is for life. Outside of two unhappy circumstances, your partner's death (Romans 7:2-3) or unfaithfulness (Matthew 5:32), you will have no second chance at marriage. This is one decision that can't be changed, even if later it turns out to be a tragic mistake.

MARRIAGE: PLEASING TO GOD AND MAN

Despite what may currently appear to be bleak prospects, most of you will eventually marry. Immediately after making man, God commented that it was not good for him to be alone; and He created the ideal partner for him (Genesis 2:18-25).

Insurance companies have compiled figures showing that

four times more bachelors than married men die of each of
the following: influenza, pneumonia, tuberculosis, suicide
and car accidents. Popular jokes to the contrary, statistics
also show that married people have far fewer headaches and
ulcers than their unmarried friends.

Most important, marriage gives a person the assurance
that someone else cares deeply about what happens to him.
It prevents him from shriveling into an individual who lives
only for himself and provides the emotional and physical
outlets everyone needs.

In a good home, "The stomach gets three meals a day and
the heart a thousand." Marriage fills in the gaps and makes
a person complete.

> *"For this cause shall a man leave his father and mother*
> *and cleave to his wife; and they twain shall be one*
> *flesh: so then they are no more twain, but one flesh.*
> *What therefore God hath joined together, let not man*
> *put asunder."*
>
> *(Mark 10:7-9)*

So the arrangement of marriage is not only pleasing to
God but good for and pleasing to man. Hopefully the opinions you form through this particular study of the Bible will
help you to eventually achieve a marriage in which you will
live "happily ever after."

TO THINK ABOUT

The following questions are intended only as mind prod-
ders and discussion starters. Many of them do not have simple right or wrong answers, but most are dealt with by
principles from the Bible. Write down your own opinion in
response to each question, and support it with scripture
whenever you can. Don't hesitate to use a concordance, top-
ical Bible or any other help in finding the verses you need.

1. Do you really feel it is essential for a teenager today to
   always obey God? What implication does this have for
   Bible study?

2. Is the "situation ethics" philosophy compatible with Christianity? Explain.
3. Show how Matthew 6:31-34 and 2 Thessalonians 3:10-12 can harmonize and both be part of a Christian's philosophy about working.
4. Is a lifestyle of "panhandling" or living off welfare to get the physical necessities justifiable?
5. Explain Paul's advice *not* to marry which is found in 1 Corinthians 7.
6. Prove by the Bible that God does approve of marriage.
7. In what specific ways could a person's married life unfavorably affect his spiritual life?
8. Think of some ways a person could serve God *better* by being married.
9. Are there any exceptions to God's "marriage for life" rule? If so, describe them; and give scriptures for them.
10. What would you personally list as advantages of being married over staying single?

DIGGING DEEPER

With most of the questions in this section it will be necessary for class members to take turns volunteering ahead of time to answer them, as they will require extra research.

1. Look up information about a religious group called the "Shakers," and tell about their unusual views on marriage.
2. Find out something about the Mormon belief in "eternal marriages." Does the Bible make any references to this, pro or con?
3. Get some current local statistics about marriage and divorce rates, plus any other related facts you can find, such as the number of children affected.

CHAPTER 2

How to Attract the Opposite Sex

"A man that hath friends must show himself friendly."

Proverbs 18:24a

You may be thinking, "It's fine to use the Bible as a source for 'religious' information; but isn't it going a little far to suggest that the Bible gives hints on how to be attractive?"

It's true, of course, that there's not a specific book in the Bible entitled "The Acts of Popularity" or "Letter to the Teenagers." But we often underestimate the wealth of wisdom in the Bible when tackling our personal problems.

Too often we classify our "religious" life as separate from our day-to-day "real" life. As a result, we rely on friends, magazines, and even "Dear Abby" for advice and overlook the handiest and most valuable guide book of all.

God assured us that His Word would "thoroughly equip us for every good work" (2 Timothy 3:16-17). If finding the right husband or wife is a "good work," (and God says in Proverbs 18:22 that it definitely is), then the Bible should furnish us some useful advice on the matter. Let's see how practical and relevant God's Word really is.

WHAT MAKES A PERSON POPULAR?

Consider for a minute—which boys in your school are the most popular? As a starter, the captain of the football team usually makes the popularity list.

It is not a girl's love of football that attracts her to the football hero, though. It is his image of strength and manliness that makes him so popular with the girls. But we don't need "98-pound weakling" ads to tell us this.

The Bible says, "The glory of young men is their strength" (Proverbs 20:29). So if boys want to build up their popularity, they can start by building up their bodies—and chalk up a point for the practical wisdom of the Bible.

Now how about girls? Have you ever known a girl who always tried to outdo anything a boy could do and who seemed to enjoy being physically superior? But how full was her date calendar?

1 Peter 3:7 points out to the wise and feminine girl that she should be "honored by men as the weaker vessel." Now Proverbs 9:13 condemns as foolish a woman who is simple-minded and helpless. And the Bible commended many women for their superior faith (Matthew 15:28), excellent judgment (Judges 4:5) and wisdom (1 Samuel 25:14-35). So we know that "weaker" does not mean "inferior."

This just means that men are designed by God to be the physically stronger—the protectors—while women are to be honored and protected. So girls, (and boys), if you would be popular, take note of God's recommendations along this line.

MIRROR, MIRROR ON THE WALL

The Bible describes the great physical beauty of such Godly women as Sarah (Genesis 12:11), Rebekah (Genesis 29:17) and Rachel (Genesis 29:17). The entire book of Song of Solomon is a poem extolling the physical attractiveness of two lovers. So we know God does not disapprove of our trying to be physically attractive. But one of the most profitable lessons we can learn from the Bible is to not judge others—or ourselves—by outward appearance alone.

It is very easy to "fall in love" with a beautiful girl or a handsome boy, but looks are too flimsy a foundation upon which to build a future. God warned that people would tend to judge others by outward appearance but that He looked at a person's heart (1 Samuel 16:7).

Anyone who has been married several years will quickly reassure you that a person's character is many times more important than his looks, and this is especially true in marriage. Notice sometime when you're in a crowd; and you will discover that the most handsome men are usually with relatively plain girls, and vice versa.

GOD'S POPULARITY COURSE

Being able to evaluate a person by what's "inside" rather than what's "outside" is a mark of real maturity. So let's look at some of the advice the Bible gives on how to be *inwardly* attractive, because this is a goal anyone can achieve (2 Corinthians 4:16).

Think first what kind of person you like for a friend. Selecting some random advice from the Scriptures, let's see what kind of friend we would construct.

First of all he or she would be thoughtful (Philippians 2:4) and kind (1 Peter 3:8). He would be genuinely thrilled when you were happy and troubled when you were sad (Romans 12:15).

If you were worried, this friend would sense it (Proverbs 20:5); and if asked, he could give you good advice (Psalms 55:14). In fact, he would be such a pleasant and uncomplaining person (Jude 16) that just being around him would make you feel better (Proverbs 17:22).

This friend would also be wise (Proverbs 4:7a), yet his wisdom would be tempered by modesty (Proverbs 27:2) and by understanding (Proverbs 4:7b). He would, of course, be a good listener (Proverbs 18:13); and you would never have to be afraid of his spreading anything you told him in confidence (Proverbs 25:19).

You could really open up and share your feelings with this person (Proverbs 11:13)—or not talk at all, if you preferred (Proverbs 17:28). If you wanted to be alone, he would understand this also (Proverbs 25:17).

Generosity would have to be another characteristic of the ideal friend (Proverbs 3:27-28), and he would be dependable and loyal (Proverbs 17:17). His reputation would be good (Proverbs 22:1); and when you were with him, you would never be embarrassed by things he might do or say (Proverbs 11:22).

GUARANTEED RESULTS

Would you be attracted to such a boy or girl and like to have this person for a close friend? Anyone would. It sounds like a Dale Carnegie graduate, doesn't it? But this is God's description of "how to win friends and influence people."

In Proverbs 3:1-4 He counsels us that if we keep His commandments, we shall be blessed with peace, a long life and *favor with both God and man.* What more could anyone ask!

TO THINK ABOUT

1. Should the ideal "girlfriend" or "boyfriend" have a different set of characteristics from the ideal friend?
2. Comment on the difference between being "popular" and "attracting attention."
3. Is there anything wrong with trying to be as physically attractive as possible? Justify your answer from the Bible.
4. Make a list of the outstanding characteristics of someone you know who is very popular with the opposite sex. Then make another list of the characteristics of someone who is unpopular datewise.
5. Define "flirting," and discuss whether it is appropriate for a Christian.
6. Is it justifiable for a Christian girl to attract boys by wearing tight sweaters, shorts, etc.? What bearing does Matthew 5:28 have on such a situation?
7. Draw up some guidelines for defining the "modest apparel" commanded in 1 Timothy 2:9.
8. In fishing, the bait used often determines what is caught. Can you apply this principle to dating?
9. What other characteristics can you think of that haven't been mentioned yet that make a person attractive to the opposite sex?
10. The Bible was written down about 2000 years ago. Does its advice still seem relevant today?

DIGGING DEEPER

1. Have several class members each ask a Christian and a non-Christian who are not members of the class to make brief lists of qualifications they consider important in a date. Then compare the lists in class.
2. Obtain a copy of Dale Carnegie's book, *How to Win Friends and Influence People.* Summarize for the class his basic rules and see how they compare with the Bible's advice.

3. List your own assets and liabilities as a date. Then select
   one of the specific traits of inner attractiveness mentioned
   in the lesson and really work on developing it during the
   next month.

CHAPTER 3

Who Shall I Date?

"Can two walk together,
except they be agreed?"

Amos 3:3

Everyone secretly dreams of being attractive and witty and captivatingly popular with the opposite sex. Everyone also goes through periods of feeling incredibly dull and ugly.

NO ANTONY OR CLEOPATRA?

Luckily, God saw to it that not only do no two people have the same fingerprints, but neither do any two people have exactly the same likes and dislikes. The same nose you see in the mirror and consider more befitting a large elephant is envied and labeled "Classic Greek" by someone else.

Have you ever watched a beauty contest and been baffled when the judges overlooked the "obvious" winner and selected the ugliest girl of all? This is just another example of the old saying, "One man's meat is another man's poison."

Remember, no one God created or for whom Christ died is unimportant. So don't underrate yourself—be a little choosey!

It is a fact that you will marry someone you date, so it makes sense to pick your dates carefully. One of them will end up being your husband or wife—forever!

BIRDS OF A FEATHER

When picking a date, it's logical to look for someone with whom you have a lot in common. Despite the current trend of tolerance towards those who are different, which is certainly a Christian attitude (Ephesians 4:2), it has been proven that people with similar backgrounds and interests get along better.

This is especially true of dating and marriage. From a practical standpoint, it will give you something to talk about on those first couple of awkward dates when it's hard to think of anything to say. This area becomes even more crucial after marraige, however.

During World War I, 10,000 American soldiers fell in love with and married girls who were perfectly nice but had different cultural backgrounds from their husbands. A follow-up study revealed that 8,000 of those 10,000 marriages ended in divorce.

The couples just didn't have enough in common. Despite the beautiful idealism of new love, the realities of daily life roughen the edges of basic differences; and soon they begin to rub and hurt.

REGARDLESS OF CREED?

One of the most basic differences a couple can have is a difference of religious beliefs. Four out of every seven Christians who marry unbelievers eventually lose their own faith.

If you were invited to go on a wonderful mountain climbing expedition but warned that four out of every seven who went would fall to their death, would you go? Equal wisdom and care must be exercised in dealing with our spiritual lives.

Consider also the fact that two-thirds of the children of interfaith marriages find the decision too difficult and consequently don't accept the faith of either parent. Even the marriage itself is more likely to fail, as the divorce rate for religiously-mixed marriages is three times higher than for marriages in which the husband and wife have the same faith. No matter how successful the surviving homes may seem, they can never be as happy as if the husband and wife were in harmony on the most important thing in life, their relationship to God.

Someone might object, "But we're just talking about dating—not marriage." The connection is worth repeating, however. You will marry someone you date! Once you're in love, cold logic takes a back seat. It's far easier to avoid unhappy situations before they develop.

NEVER ON SUNDAY

Not until it's too late does one really understand the many conflicts which arise from marrying a person who doesn't share your concern for Christ and the church—problems such as what to do on weekends, which friends to invite to your home, where to go on evenings out, the religious education of your children, and on and on.

Only a parent can understand the difficulty of getting children up and fed and dressed and taking them to church while Daddy or Mommy is still in bed. How can a person who is devoted to putting Christ first in his life ever purposely so handicap himself by becoming permanently tied to filling the desires of an unbeliever?

God was thinking of our own happiness, as well as our eternal destiny, when He advised us "Be not unequally yoked with an unbeliever" (2 Corinthians 6:14-15). This verse applies to more than marriage; but to exclude marriage would be an injustice, for what is a more binding "yoke" or "fellowship" than marriage?

Solomon was the wisest man who ever lived. He wrote three of the most inspiring books of the Bible. Yet when he ignored God's advice and married women who did not worship as he did, even Solomon weakened and turned away from God (1 Kings 11:1-6).

Consider also that "the unbeliever makes God a liar" (1 John 5:10). How would your *earthly* father feel if you married someone who called him a liar?

BUT THERE ISN'T ANYONE

The problem is that sometimes there just aren't any other Christians to date, and this is certainly a valid point. The most common solution is to just date whoever is available—usually someone you meet at school.

This probably beats being a social recluse, as long as you use good judgment. For example, if a Christian were to date someone who enjoys drinking, either the Christian will have to give in and drink or the two will be constantly arguing.

But assuming the Christian dates a non-Christian with similar high morals, the one important thing to remember is to talk to your date about Christ as soon as possible. The Bible says that we must always be ready to tell others about "the hope that is within us" (1 Peter 3:15).

The longer you wait, the harder this becomes. Study, pray and then plunge in! If you really care for your date, it will be impossible *not* to share with him the abundant life you have found in Christ, (John 10:10). And if he or she is driven off by hearing about Christ, he is definitely not the kind of date you want anyway (Romans 1:21-22).

If there are eligible boys or girls in your own congregation but they just don't seem interested, another possibility is to try whipping up some enthusiasm. Good congregational spirit, even among teenagers, has to be cultivated.

Stage a real campaign of enjoyable mixed parties. Sure, it's a challenge; but make your parties so much fun that even the most stubborn will want to come. Plan lively games to get the boys and girls together. Be sensitive to what works and what doesn't. Then get a good friend to arrange the next get-together. Eventually, nature will take its course.

But what if *you* are the disinterested one because there aren't any desirable possibilities in your congregation? Then get a sympathetic adult to back you and organize some monthly get-togethers for the young people of all the area congregations. This should widen your horizons considerably. Teenage devotionals, skating or bowling parties, banquets, campouts, hayrides—all of these have proven to be successful get acquainted opportunities.

HANG IN THERE!

If all fails, don't give up! The really big opportunity is still to come, and that's a Christian college.

Don't be mislead. Anyone who is willing to work can afford to go to a Christian college. There you will find a thousand or more unmarried Christians your age—half of them the opposite sex!

In your favor, by then your own personal dating poise will be much more developed—as well as the attitudes and ambitions of those you'll date—thus giving both of you a better basis for evaluating possible lifetime partners.

One final plug—while the national divorce rate is now over 25%, married couples who met at a Christian college have a divorce rate of only ½ of 1%.

YOUR BEST ALLY

Most important, don't forget to ask for God's help in this important matter. Remember how Abraham's servant asked for and received God's help in finding a good wife for Isaac (Genesis 24)? God has promised to help us whenever we ask (John 15:7). Let's give Him a try!

TO THINK ABOUT

1. Can you relate 1 Corinthians 10:31 to dating and choosing a husband or wife?
2. Is it true that "opposites attract," and do "opposites" make good dates?
3. 1 Corinthians 7:39 says that if a widow remarries, it must be "only in the Lord." What do you think are the reasons for this restriction, and could these same reasons also apply to young people who have never been married?
4. Locate some Old Testament scriptures showing God's feelings about religiously-mixed marriages.
5. Besides the possibility of marriage, what are some other potential dangers when dating non-Christians?
6. Role play some approaches for talking to a non-Christian date about Christ.
7. List some specific arguments that might occur "after the honeymoon is over" in a home where a Christian is married to a non-Christian.
8. Does the Bible say anything which would relate to racially mixed marriages?
9. What are the pro's and con's of accepting blind dates?
10. Pretending you are a parent, write down the qualifications you would like to see in the people your child dates.

DIGGING DEEPER

1. Ask three Christians who are married to unbelievers to give you their honest advice about your marrying someone who is not a Christian.
2. Secure and read to the class a copy of the Roman Catholic Ante-Nuptial Contract and Promises.
3. Bring to class samples of the aids your congregation has for helping teach others about Christ, such as filmstrips, charts, videos or tracts.

CHAPTER 4

Where Can We Go?

"Prove all things; hold fast
that which is good. Abstain
from all appearance of evil."
1 Thessalonians 5:21-22

After the "who" of dating is taken care of, the next most important question is "where" to go on the date.

Have you ever known someone who seemed to think "fun" automatically meant "wrong"? During the first century when the Jews were under Roman occupation, it is true that very few places existed where Christians could go for pleasure. The "in" entertainments of the day were immoral pagan celebrations or cruel Roman extravaganzas such as feeding Christians to lions.

Because recreation took such terrible forms in those days, many Christians began to look upon recreation as sinful and abhorrent; and a remnant of this attitude remains in some religious people today. But an open-minded study of the Bible would not support the belief that religion is synonymous with dullness and stuffiness. Quite the opposite!

HAPPINESS IS CHRISTIANITY

God's Word rings with phrases such as "rejoice," "be joyful" and "be glad." Jesus often took time out to relax or enjoy a feast with friends. He certainly never came across as stuffy or boring. He even referred to His Way as the "more abundant life" (John 10:10b).

An activity should never be labeled wrong simply because it is enjoyable, but only if it comes between you and your responsibility to God. So let's consider some things Christian young people can enjoy doing on dates.

Often you'll find it an advantage to double date with other Christian couples. This will provide more interesting ideas of what to do, prevent you from getting "out of circulation," and avoid the dangers of just the two of you being alone all the time.

Group date possibilities are unlimited. How many of the following activities have you tried lately?

Making homemade ice cream, miniature golf, sunrise breakfast, hayride, bicycle hike, ice skating, barbecue, fishing (sure, girls like to fish!), a progressive dinner, visiting a country fair, golfing or a driving range, rent a video, window shopping in the mall, backwards party, dress-up catered banquet, records and relaxing party (after test week), table games, "Come-as-you-are," taffy pull, surprise birthday party, lawn games, scavenger hunt, home movies, TV and popcorn, Sadie Hawkins party (girls ask boys), steak fry or weiner roast, depending on your budget, horseback riding, board games, hobo party and cookout, skiing, bowling, tubing or tobogganing, zoo, amusement park, free sight-seeing tours, an overnight campout, masquerade party, free local exhibits, parents-vs.-kids night (playing games, that is), charades, Polynesian luau, Mexican supper, watermelon feed, tennis, a musical hootenanny, a banana split party.

. . . THE SPICE OF LIFE

Surely a few of those possibilities will get your imagination in gear! Of course, not all dates need to be spent in play. Visiting an elderly person in a nursing home or giving a Halloween party for the younger children is enjoyable for everyone involved.

Several couples can have lots of fun repainting a Bible school classroom or scrubbing the church's bus. Work is always more rewarding, and sometimes even more fun, than a purely "pleasure-type" endeavor.

Besides, it is very important that occasionally your dates are of the informal "wash-the-car-in-jeans" variety. Seeing each other only in dressed-up, continually structured situations will not give you a fair chance to really get to know one another; and getting to know one another is one of the main purposes of dating.

Even staying home dates are sometimes a treat after a hectic week—as long as you don't limit home just to the sofa. Try inviting another couple over to make waffles or tacos. Cooking them, eating them and cleaning up after them makes a fun, full evening.

Some of the best dates of all are the impromptu kinds when one person just says, "Bring someone and come over after church." It's not really important who brings whom or what you do—the best part is just getting together for fun and to get to know one another. The serious just-you-and-me dates can always come later.

DANGER ZONES

A few places you could go on a date are not wrong in themselves but can be a bad choice because of related problems. For example, a Christian couple would show wisdom in avoiding such places as lonely back rows at drive-in movies or remote "scenic" spots in the country. Another inherently innocent situation to get out of would be a school party at which marijuana shows up, or a picnic when someone arrives with a keg of beer.

Since the possibility has been brought up of there being some wrong places to go on a date, let's go ahead and consider the criteria for determining what a Christian should and should not do in the area of recreation.

Popularity, personal taste, the preacher's opinion—none of these are the basis for deciding what is right and what is wrong. But the Bible *is* a valid basis, and it gives many guidelines in this area. Examine the following dozen questions:

1. Does the Bible condemn it specifically or in principle? (John 12:48)
2. Can I do it "to the glory of God?" (1 Corinthians 10:31)
3. Would Jesus do it? (1 Peter 2:21)
4. Does it enhance my image as a Christian? (1 Timothy 4:12)

5. Is it harmful to my body? (1 Corinthians 6:19-20)
6. Does it infringe on God's share of my time, talents or money? (Matthew 6:33)
7. Might it be a bad influence on weaker Christians? (1 Corinthians 8:9-13)
8. Is it questionable? (Romans 14:23, 1 Thessalonians 5:22)
9. Does it cause me to associate with unwholesome people? (2 Corinthians 6:14-17)
10. Would I mind if everyone knew I did it? (Ecclesiastes 12:14)
11. Does it adversely affect the rights or property of others? (Matthew 7:12)
12. Does it lift or lower me spiritually? (Romans 8:5-6)

It is very important to stop and look up each of the scriptures just listed in order to be convinced that they are really principles laid down by God and not just a cut-and dried list in a Bible class workbook. Then choose a sample activity and put it to the test.

GOD'S LAWS—FOR HIS BENEFIT OR OURS?

Each person owes it to himself to attempt to be unbiased and honest in his evaluation of any question (Proverbs 15:28). It's always easy to find something wrong with things we don't like to do anyway; but it takes an extremely honest, open-minded person to recognize wrong in something we really want to do.

Sometimes young people long to break loose and be free to do whatever they want, but genuine freedom comes only with compliance to the will of God (John 8:32, 17:17b, Galatians 5:1). God didn't give us the Bible just to show who was boss.

God made not only us but the entire universe and all its laws. He can look down from a viewpoint which is unbiased, except by love, and see clearly what will work out best for us, physically as well as spiritually. God's laws are for *our* good, not His; and the realization of this will increase with spiritual maturity.

THE BEST THINGS IN LIFE . . .

One last suggestion—cultivate an enjoyment of simple things! Teenage boys seldom have much money; and what they do earn, they are usually trying to save for a car or college.

Give them a break, girls, and occasionally offer to pack a picnic lunch, or suggest doing something together which doesn't cost anything, like attending a free concert in the park. When he starts thinking in terms of a wife, expensive tastes will certainly not be one of his requirements.

Remember, the object of dating is to have fun and to get to know one another. *Any* where that will fill these two essentials and pass the dozen criteria listed earlier is a great "where" for a date.

TO THINK ABOUT

1. Select an activity you are not sure whether a Christian should engage in, and then apply "The Dozen Test" to it. Write down which principles, if any, make it wrong.
2. Can an activity be right within itself but be made wrong because of circumstances? If so, explain; and give an example.
3. Whose responsibility is it to plan wholesome recreation for Christian young people?
4. How does "*I* don't see anything wrong with it" rate as a basis for determining right and wrong? Find some scriptures which relate to this.
5. Many recreations, skiing, for example, are not even mentioned in the Bible. So how can you use the Bible to determine whether they are right or wrong?
6. Do you feel sorry for Christians when it comes to recreation and having fun? Why?
7. Discuss the implications on the area of recreation of the following two scriptures:
   1 Corinthians 8:9-13
   1 Thessalonians 5:21-22
8. Tell about some Bible characters who had the courage to

say "no" when a proposed activity violated their beliefs.
9. How strong an argument is "Everybody's doing it?" Quote some Bible verses which apply.
10. Do you agree that God gives us laws "for our own good?" Give some examples.

DIGGING DEEPER

1. See if you can dig up any information on a Calvinist religious group led by Philip Jacob Spener known as "Pietists." State and disprove their beliefs about recreation.
2. Using role playing, demonstrate some diplomatic ways of saying "no" to questionable activities. Remember, you must not compromise your principles (Romans 14:23). Yet neither do you want to be self-righteous or offensive (Matthew 10:16).
3. Have you and your family done anything personally to provide recreation for the church teenagers? If not, write down a couple of possible ideas, one of which you will really try to do within the next three months.

CHAPTER 5

How Do Parents Fit In?

"My son, hear the instruction of thy father, and forsake not the law of thy mother."

Proverbs 1:8

Not only do young people have to get along with their *own* parents, but it helps tremendously if they get along with their date's parents. To some teenagers, agreeing with parents is practically like committing treason. Asking their advice, or accepting it, is equivalent to that awful sin of actually *needing* parents.

One of the surest signs of maturity, however, is the ability to listen to others. It isn't necessary, or even sensible, to *agree* with all the advice one gets; but a wise person is not afraid to listen to the suggestions of others, even parents. He has the confidence to discuss things with his parents and accept any good advice he hears.

Of course, parents also need reminders about how to get along better with their children. But since they'll probably never read any of this, the situation will have to be approached from your angle.

THE GENERATION GAP—GOOD OR BAD?

As long as children live at home and are supported by their parents, it is typical and even legal for their parents to "legislate" in such dating areas as where, when, how many, how late and even with whom.

Some conflicting opinions will always exist between parents and teenagers, due to differences in personality, age, experience and goals. But God has made it clear that parents

23

are to guide and discipline their children. They have no choice—if they love God and their children (Proverbs 3:12). Read the sad condemnation of the old priest, Eli, in 1 Samuel 3:12-13, simply because "he did not restrain" his sons.

It is also clear that God expects children to respect and obey their parents (Ephesians 6:1-3). Deuteronomy 21:18-21 paints a rather fearful picture of how God feels about disobedient children.

In those days, rebellious children were taken out and stoned to death by the men of the city! God leaves no room for debate on whether we have to go along with our parents' wishes—we must. But we can discuss some ways to make this more of a pleasure and less of a pain.

NOBODY TRUSTS ME

One of the biggest complaints of teenagers is that they would like, and usually deserve, more trust. (It is also interesting, however, that one of parents' biggest complaints is that their teens show too little trust in *them*.) How do you get your parents to trust you more and thus gain more freedom and privileges?

The Bible points out that he who is dependable in that which is least is also dependable in much (Luke 16:10). That's pretty much how parents view the situation too.

If a person can't be depended on to get his dirty socks into the clothes hamper, how can he be dependable enough to be trusted out alone with the car? There are lots of easy ways to prove your ability to handle more independence, such as getting your homework done well and on time without reminders, being honest about where you're going and with whom, taking good care of your clothes or voluntarily pitching in with some of the work around the house. These are foolproof methods of alerting your parents to your readiness for more trust and freedom.

Naturally when parents *do* start allowing some special privileges, these must be guarded carefully. For example, a boy should always tell a girl's parents about when he expects to bring her home and have their approval. Then he'd better get her there by that time, if he values their opinion of him—as well as future privileges for her.

Of course, there will always be ball games that run late and the traditional flat tire; but there will also always be telephones with which to call home and explain. Not until you're a parent yourself will you understand how long and fearful 30 minutes late can seem!

Another good way to build trust for yourself is by inviting your friends to your house. Unwillingness to do this makes parents think that either your friends are unwholesome or you are ashamed of your family, and neither conclusion does much to improve family relations.

PARENTS ARE PEOPLE TOO

Disillusionment is another common problem between teenagers and parents. Young children idealize their parents. Their mother is always the prettiest in the world, and their dad is the strongest.

But with the increasing knowledge of the teenage years comes the jolting realization that parents have their share of weaknesses and inconsistencies. Some teenagers respond indignantly and somewhat self-righteously by swinging to the opposite extreme and scorning *everything* their parents do. A really mature person, however, realizes and accepts that all people, including parents and even himself, have small and large faults and hypocrisies (1 John 1:8).

There is so much bad in the best of us,
And so much good in the worst of us;
That it ill behooves any of us,
To find fault with the rest of us.

It helps to remember that parents are just outgrown teenagers themselves. Giving birth to a child doesn't automatically provide a person with extra wisdom, although all parents wish it would. You will wish it yourself someday when you have teenage children of your own who find *you* unreasonable and hopelessly out of touch with reality.

Ephesians 4:32 teaches "Be ye kind . . . , tenderhearted, forgiving one another. . . ." Why is it easier to practice this with strangers than with those in our own family?

But Christian principles are needed even more inside the

home than outside of it, for in our home we tend to relax the good manners and inhibitions which temper our contacts with casual acquaintances. An excellent conscience prodder is to read 1 Corinthians 13:4-7, inserting the phrase, "In my home I. . . ."

DRAGONS AND EASTER BUNNIES

The tendency of young people to be easily swayed is one reason parents occasionally resist when their children want to start dating and driving. A small child will believe in anything, including fire-snorting dragons and Easter bunnies.

Teens, too, are still sometimes inclined to be too easily persuaded by new philosophies and fads. Open-mindedness is an excellent virtue, but should not be confused with gullibleness. Ephesians 4:14 describes those who swallow every new teaching that comes along as "childish."

Change can be, but is not automatically, good. Your parents must be convinced that you have the wisdom and courage to not be easily overcome by every influence you encounter when away from them (Proverbs 14:15-16). Moderation and good judgment in relation to current fashion fads is one way to demonstrate this.

By the time you're old enough to date, you're also probably smart enough to have already figured out many of the "rules" for getting along with your particular parents and earning the increased freedom you now need. But keep in mind the following hints for effective parent-teen communications.

1. Be willing to compromise—don't let pride make you stubborn.
2. Avoid pouting and playing the martyr.
3. Tears or tantrums only reinforce their doubts about your maturity.
4. Don't stoop to sarcasm—this ends effective communication.
5. Remember that parents have pride too—leave them an "out."
6. Always "keep your cool," even though parents are often guilty of losing their tempers first.

7. Reserve a little time just for your family. (They once had first place in your life—it hurts to give you up all at once!)
8. Avoid picking petty quarrels with brothers and sisters. Learn the mature art of ignoring some things.
9. Limit the use of current slang when trying to persuade parents.
10. Voluntarily share some things with them, such as details of a party or how school is going.

If you have the misfortune of coming from a genuinely unjust and unChristian home, try to learn from it (Romans 8:28). Make it strengthen you (2 Corinthians 12:10). Jesus asked us to be willing to endure hard times for Him (2 Timothy 2:3). Pray about it—perhaps God is using this trial to prepare you for a special job for Him!

CUTTING THE APRON STRINGS

Have you ever in a moment of anger considered leaving home, and then suddenly realized what all you'd be giving up? God meant for each of us to have a home. We need one, and any give and take necessary to live peaceably in your home is well worth the trouble.

Because of their love for you, your parents will sometimes be too strict. But it is concern and not curiosity that makes them wait up until you get home.

Remember, God told us to honor and obey our parents "That it may be well with thee, and thou mayest live long on the earth" (Ephesians 6:2-3). That's a pretty good incentive!

TO THINK ABOUT

1. Imagine that you are a psychologist, and analyze why you think parents and their children often see things so differently.
2. List some ways young people may reveal immaturity and thus lose privileges.
3. Now list some specific ways of demonstrating maturity.
4. What should you do if the will of your parents differs

from the will of God? Give some scriptures proving your
stand.

5. Does all responsibility to parents end at marriage? Has
   God given us any criteria in this matter?
6. What practical advice can be gained from Ephesians 4:14
   and Proverbs 14:15?
7. If your parents have made what you consider to be a
   totally unreasonable and unfair decision, is there anything you can do about it?
8. What two restrictions does Ephesians 6:4 place on parents?
9. List some dating rules of your family and compare them
   with those of other families represented in the class.
10. What are some of the advantages to a teenager of having
    parents?

DIGGING DEEPER

1. List five main complaints about your parents, trying to
   name the worst one first. Then ask your parents to write
   down their five main complaints about you. In class, tally
   and discuss the results.
2. Read and talk about the attitudes revealed by (a) Isaac to
   his father in Genesis 22:1-13, (b) Esther to her uncle in
   Esther 2:20, 4:1-16 and (c) Jephthah's daughter to her fa-
   ther in Judges 11:30-40 when they were each facing diffi-
   cult situations regarding obedience and disobedience.
3. Look up the following proverbs and summarize the par-
   ent-child advice found in each:
   Proverbs 1:8
   Proverbs 3:12
   Proverbs 6:20
   Proverbs 10:1
   Proverbs 13:1
   Proverbs 13:24
   Proverbs 15:5
   Proverbs 15:32
   Proverbs 22:6
   Proverbs 23:22
   Proverbs 28:7
   Proverbs 30:17

CHAPTER 6

Dating Etiquette for Christians

"Finally, be ye all of one mind, having compassion one of another, love as brethren, be sympathetic, be courteous."

1 Peter 3:8

To be preoccupied with etiquette for its own sake would be superficial and foolish. Young people particularly place a high premium on sincerity and being oneself, and hypocrisy has always been distasteful—even more so to God than to men (Isaiah 29:13). But while etiquette in a formal sense is an established set of rules governing social conduct, in a deeper sense it actually revolves around such basics of Christianity as thoughtfulness, unselfishness and respect.

LOVE SAYS IT ALL

Christianity, which is a religion based on love, should have little need for excessive rules on how to treat others. Love says it all (Matthew 22:39-40).

Yet the Bible also advises us to submit to the ordinances of man for God's sake (1 Peter 2:13). Paul said that he tried to become all things to all men in an effort to win others to Christ (1 Corinthians 9:22). This is a very important principle.

A Christian is not one who "bucks the system" just to show he is his own boss (Philippians 2:3-5). In fact, because of his lack of concern with himself and his genuine concern for others, he willingly bends his wishes to avoid offending his fellowman (Romans 14:15-21; 1 Corinthians 8:9-13), refusing only when it would conflict with the law of God (Acts 4:18-20).

DON'T BE "PIGGISH"

Christian youth usually do not find the so-called rules of etiquette inhibitive or cumbersome but rather a natural outgrowth of their religion in practice. Etiquette simply means knowing the right thing to do and when to do it. A synonym for etiquette is "discretion," and Proverbs 11:22 states that a person without discretion is like a jewel in a pig's nose.

Even the Old Testament had rules to help people know what to do when. For example, Leviticus 19:32 told the Israelites to rise when an elderly person entered. So let's mention some of the most common rules of etiquette which apply to the area of dating.

For those of you who already date a lot, this may seem elementary. But try to remember the butterflies of insecurity you felt on the night of your first date, and then laugh and bear with us.

ONE STEP AT A TIME

Let's start with setting up the date. Probably the boy will telephone, this being the least terrifying way to ask a girl for a date. After checking the clock first to make sure it isn't too early or too late or mealtime—people "in love" often lose all track of time—make the call.

Hopefully the first voice he hears will not respond rudely, "Who is this?" Should he have the bad luck to get up his nerve and call and then find the girl is not home, he should leave his name and then call back later, as it is still a bit awkward for girls to call boys.

If his prospective date comes to the phone, however, after a minimum of small talk he should get to the point. This is particularly important if she indicates she is busy, which most people are (Proverbs 25:17). It is amazing how thick normally bright people can be when it comes to catching a hint over the telephone.

Now if the girl says "yes," he's in luck—the worst is over! Briefly give details such as time and where you'll be going, so she'll know how to dress, and then close off. Saying good-by is the responsibility of the one who makes the call.

DON'T GIVE UP TOO EASILY

If she says "no," etiquette allows asking her out again on two other occasions. Even God taught us not to give up too easily (Luke 11:5-10). But, except under unusual circumstances, call it quits after three consecutive "no's."

Girls, if you'd really like to go but can't, don't be afraid to show it—it will help the poor guy's pride. But if you are sure you never care to go out with him, try to kindly cue him in and spare him further embarrassment. This can be done by not giving much of an excuse and not overplaying the sorry part.

One other warning, boys. Ask her in plenty of time, so she won't feel like a last resort for the girl you asked earlier who came down with chicken pox!

COLLECT YOURSELF . . . AND YOUR DATE

Assuming you've gotten a date and the time has arrived, the boy should pick up his date at her home, (not at a friend's or in the front of the movie.) Admittedly, the meeting-her-parents-and-helping-her-on-with-her-coat-under-their-watchful-eyes ordeal can be unnerving, but it is just one of those responsibilities that goes along with the privilege of being old enough to date.

PARENTAL PROTOCOL

Speaking of parents, it will start you off on a better foot if you don't arrive late (or too early, either) or in a fanfare of screeching brakes and roaring exhaust pipes. And if the girl has much self-respect—or parents—you'd better plan on going up to the door rather than just honking.

Girls, it's your job to handle the introductions, which will necessitate your being ready on time. An easy rule for simplifying introductions is to always say the oldest or most honored person's name first (Romans 13:7), e.g., "Mom, this is Brad." It will also get things rolling better if you throw in a conversation starter, such as, "Dad, Brad is on the debate squad."

To be on the safe side, always call older people by their last names unless asked to do otherwise. (Many younger "old" people do prefer to be called by their first names.) Now, if you've survived all that, let's get on with the date itself.

WHO DOES WHAT WHEN?

Let's pretend you're going to eat out, since that involves several different rules of etiquette. At really nice restaurants, an attendant may park your car and another offer to check your coat, for which they will expect to be tipped later.

It is polite to wait until the host arrives to seat you, and the girl should follow him first to the table. If the host does not seat the girl, her date should do so. On double dates, all boys remain standing until the girls are seated; but girls may sit down as soon as they get to the table.

As for ordering, it is customary in fancy restaurants for the boy to ask his date what she'd like and then give her order to the waiter himself. If he or she doesn't know this, though, it would be a much worse breach of etiquette to make an issue of it. Remember, etiquette in practice always goes by what makes the other person feel comfortable (Matthew 7:12).

HOT DOGS OR STEAK?

In ordering, the girl takes her cue from her date. If he selects the roast beef dinner, it would be just as awkward for her to order a coke and hot dog as to order the top steak on the menu.

From then on, just enjoy the meal! Should further service be necessary, don't hesitate to ask for it; but get your waiter's attention by politely saying "Sir" or "Miss" and avoid finger snapping or whistling.

After the meal, always leave a tip. Usually 15% or more is expected. By observing other diners, boys can determine whether to pay at the table or go to a cash register. Girls, now is the time to excuse yourself and add some lipstick if necessary—in the restroom.

IT'S ON THE HOUSE

If you're eating in someone's home, naturally the rules are more relaxed. Here, thoughtfulness is the cue.

Go to the dining room immediately when your hostess says the meal is ready. Seat the lady next to you, and then wait to sit and then to begin eating until the hostess does.

Don't forget to compliment her several times during and after the meal (Proverbs 25:11). For a really special occasion, it is nice to take a small gift, such as flowers or candy, and write a brief but sincere thank-you note afterwards. Remember the lesson on gratitude Jesus taught in Luke 17:11-18.

One final hint can be taken from 1 Corinthians 10:27, which states simply, "Whatever is set before you, eat. . . ." (And you thought only your parents said that!)

SUNDAY MANNERS

This might be a good time to consider one other phase of dating etiquette, and that is how to act in worship services (1 Timothy 3:15). Have you ever sat behind a new Mama and Papa who were thoroughly entertained by their new little offspring all during the service? Perhaps you wondered why they even bothered to come.

It's awfully easy to notice such errors of indiscretion in others, but much harder to notice our own. Yet wouldn't this be similar to the dating couple who cuddle and coo at each other throughout the worship service?

Most people are not offended by quiet hand-holding during services or a casual arm on the pew behind a girl, but anything heavier than this shows very poor taste and a lack of respect for God and your date (Proverbs 11:22).

Analyze your reasons for going to church. Each of us needs to occasionally stop and contemplate the magnitude and jealousy of our God (Deuteronomy 6:15). Christ emphasized that we must love Him more than all others—even boyfriends and girlfriends—in order to be worthy of Him (Matthew 10:37).

Don't allow yourself the easy out of sitting at the back where you can't be seen. Experience the joy of wholeheartedly worshiping God with one you care about, and never date someone with whom you cannot feel close to God (Amos 3:3).

HOW BRIGHT IS YOUR LIGHT?

Despite the thousands of do's and don't's of textbook etiquette, they all still come back to the one basic Christian attitude of concern for others. Bad manners are just an outward symptom of a selfish heart.

It is often pointed out how strenuous it must be for the President and his wife to be continually observed. But in a very real sense, Christians are in the same position. Christ likened us to "the salt of the earth," "cities set on hills" and "lights of the world" (Matthew 5:13-16). As Christians, we are also on continual display. We must be careful that our social actions brighten rather than dim our lights.

TO THINK ABOUT

1. Is observing good manners just another form of "knuckling under to The Establishment?"
2. Some rules of etiquette seem needlessly tedious, such as which fork to use when. Is there any valid purpose for such rules?
3. Give a few examples of when it would be best to take exception to the established rules of proper etiquette.
4. Do you agree that most of our "manners" are based on thoughtfulness? Give some illustrations.
5. Do you think the Women's Liberation movement will have an effect on our current rules of etiquette? If so, how?
6. Discuss the practical meanings of the word "discretion."
7. In the area of "church manners," what are some of your own pet peeves?
8. Analyze why you think people sit near the back during a church service.
9. What traits do you feel characterize a good and bad guest? The Bible says a great deal about *being* hospitable (*having* guests), but does it say anything that would apply to being one?
10. Do you agree with the statement that "love makes all other rules unnecessary"? Demonstrate why or why not.

DIGGING DEEPER

1. Make a list of some other "rules" of dating etiquette, including any local customs, which you think are important that haven't been mentioned in this lesson.
2. Can you find any Old or New Testament examples or customs which are similar to any of our current rules of etiquette?
3. For your own "social security" and confidence, check out and read a current, nationally-accepted etiquette book. See if you can discover anything you didn't know.

Chapter 7

Potential Pitfalls

"Don't let the world around you squeeze you into its own mold, but let God remold your minds from within, so that you may prove in practice that the plan of God for you is good, meets all his demands and moves toward the goal of true maturity."
Romans 12:2, (Phillips version)

We have already considered a few potential pitfalls of dating, such as dating people you wouldn't want to marry or trying to base popularity on "sex appeal." In this chapter and the next we'll discuss a few more possible problem areas. One of these areas is when to start dating.

EARLY DATING

When your parents were young, it was generally accepted that dating didn't begin until the age of 16. Then junior high students appeared on the dating scene, and now it is not too uncommon for sixth and even fifth graders to date.

So what are the pro's and con's of getting an early start? An advocate might argue, "The younger one starts dating, the more years of experience he will get. Thus he will be in a better position to evaluate and pick a marriage partner." But the facts don't work out that way.

Statistics show that in most cases the younger a person starts dating, the younger he will marry. So he doesn't get more experience after all. He just gets it sooner, and when he's not quite as preapred to benefit from it.

The teenage divorce rate is three times higher than the national average. Three out of every four teenage marriages end in divorce, and these are very poor odds.

BUT I PREFER OLDER BOYS

Since girls usually mature much earlier than boys, a 12-year-old girl would have to date a boy of 16 or 17, to date her equal in physical maturity. But the emotional and intellectual differences made by those four years are tremendous.

You may think, "But my dad is five years older than my mom; and they get along fine." As people grow older, age differences do fade in importance. But how much do you have in common with a brother or sister who is five years younger than you? Obviously, you are much more sophisticated in practically every way (1 Corinthians 13:11).

With real effort, they could "act" like you temporarily and do the things you do. But it would be unnatural and unfair for them to have to give up the pleasures of their own age and level of maturity.

In a similar way, girls who date in their very early teens are forced to date older boys. This causes them to miss a whole wonderful segment of their lives—their young and carefree teens—in order to compete in the more serious world of the older teen.

Dating too early forces an unripe maturity. We all know what happens when a flower is pried open before its petals are ready to open naturally.

It is sometimes the ambition and competitiveness of parents which drives children to start dating before they are really ready. But youth is a precious, never-again commodity; hoard it stingily.

The ability to live in the present and enjoy "now" fully is an enviable talent which many people of 40 have never mastered (Ecclesiastes 9:7-10). Those early teenage years are custom made for a carefree and exuberant enjoyment of life (Ecclesiastes 11:9).

GOING STEADY

Most situations have their good points and their bad points, and going steady is no exception. You will have to determine what is best for you in your particular circumstances. First let's consider the advantages of going steady.

ADVANTAGES

What girl would deny the thrill of wearing that big bulky letter sweater and having his class ring wrapped with tape on her finger? And boys have to admit it's kind of nice to wear her dainty little ring on a chain around his neck and have her eagerly waiting for him after school. It's an ego booster and a status symbol saying "I'm popular—somebody likes me very much!"

From a practical standpoint, going steady is also excellent date insurance—no waiting by the phone for a date to the big party. And you do get to know a person very well. It is also financially advantageous, as each date needn't be such a big production.

DISADVANTAGES

But going steady obviously limits dating experience and often leads to the feeling of having missed something. The fewer people one dates, the less chance he will have to get to know people and decide what characteristics are most important to him in selecting a lifetime "steady."

If you start steadily dating one person when you're 15 and nothing severe enough to break off the relationship occurs, you may end up marrying that person. It's not that the two of you are perfectly matched for each other. It's just a fact of life that if a boy and girl halfway like each other and are together enough, eventually force of habit takes over and physical desires develop until the logical conclusion is marriage.

At 15 had you begun going steady with a different person, you would probably have married that one. Shining knights and white horses to the contrary, there is usually more "chance" than "fate" involved in determining who marries whom (Ecclesiastes 9:11).

You deserve the chance to date enough people to make a discriminating choice before you settle down to going steady. Of course, the chances can be considerably improved in your favor by praying, as Eliezer did, that God will guide you in finding a good husband or wife (Genesis 24:12-14).

DON'T FENCE ME IN

Another danger of going steady is that of crowding each other too much too soon. Usually steadies take each other pretty much for granted and are together much of the time.

Naturally this is time consuming and has its effect on outside interests, such as schoolwork and particularly other friendships. Frequently one of the partners begins to feel boxed in and wants out, ruining what might have been a good relationship under less cramped conditions (Proverbs 25:17).

Sometimes two people are sort of thrown together by others and considered to be going steady, when actually neither of them had that in mind. But boys have an unwritten loyalty code about other boys' girls; so it you have any hopes of dating someone else, take pains not to let yourself get too closely labeled with just one person.

If necessary, get your girlfriend to bribe her brother into taking you out—just to let others know you're still available. As Ann Landers put it: "Going steady is like settling for one outfit when you could have twenty."

THERE'S TOM, DICK . . . AND
HARRY'S NOT BAD EITHER

Being "in love with love" is a delightful but deceptive situation. Infatuation appears suddenly; love requires time and effort.

Of course, a time will come when you are genuinely in love; and neither of you will desire to date others. But if you would still sort of like to try dating someone else, should someone better come along, going steady would be an unwise and dishonest involvement for you at this time. So think it over objectively before you commit yourself.

PETTING

A discussion of going steady often leads to the topic of petting. In order to effectively discuss this subject, it will help to stop and define terms.

Quoting from Ann Landers again, "Necking is an exchange of hugs and kisses, keeping all hands on deck and all feet on the floor. Petting is, in general, necking out of control."

Others claim that "necking" involves only from the neck up. For our purposes, let's consider petting to be a little more than a goodnight kiss or hug but not so much as going to bed with a date, which will be discussed in a later chapter.

A MEANS TO AN END

What about "petting" for a Christian? Obviously it is enjoyable. God Himself made physical desire and pleasures a part of us (Genesis 1:28a, Hebrews 13:4a).

Petting is exciting, and it makes us feel desirable. But it also arouses strong feelings which are not to be satisfied outside of marriage (1 Corinthians 6:9-10).

Petting is nature's way of preparing a couple to enjoy unlimited and fulfilling passion. Any time one crosses nature—in this case by petting but stopping before the natural conclusion—he will suffer.

The tensions of aroused but unfulfilled sexual desires are not easily dealt with. The habit of heavy petting and "stopping in time" can even cause sexual problems later in marriage.

An even more serious problem is that, despite best intentions, petting is a road meant to go somewhere, and sometimes people get started down that road and can't stop. Right or wrong, emotions usually win out over intellect.

In other words, if you *feel* strongly about something at the moment, it becomes easy to rationalize away everything you've ever been taught about it. The millions of illegitimate children in the world are forceful testimony against the "I'll-stop-in-time" philosophy.

"But what's wrong with petting as long as I make *sure* that things never get completely out of control?" someone might ask. Assuming that such is possible—that a person could be so totally intellectually geared that his emotions never interfered—there is still another factor which makes petting wrong.

Matthew 5:27-29 teaches that if we get to the point where we wish we could go all the way with our date, we are guilty of adultery—even if we don't allow it to happen physically. In this situation, a person is not only responsible for himself but also for his date. If your petting leads your date to sin by his thoughts, you will be held guilty also (Matthew 18:6-8).

IS THIS LOVE?

Petting also makes it very difficult to objectively evaluate your date as a possible marriage partner. It blinds those involved to possibly grave incompatibilities in other areas.

Passion's most insidious trait is its ability to mask as love. Many homes have been begun on the basis of strong physical attraction and have then come to a bitter end when everyday living revealed the shallowness of such a foundation.

Another of the bad effects of petting is that it causes guilt. Christians know that sex is special and reserved for marriage (1 Corinthians 7:1-2, 9, 36). With this knowledge, one can't pet heavily and feel good about it afterwards (James 4:17).

Guilt requires a heavy toll—physically and emotionally (Psalms 31:10). It cuts into a person's self-respect, nags at his conscience, and stifles spirituality.

PETTING AND POPULARITY

But can a girl who won't pet hope to be popular? A questionnaire given to students at the University of California, Michigan State and Cornell revealed almost unanimously that it is not essential for a girl to pet to be popular.

Of course, there are *some* boys with whom a girl would have to pet to be popular. But a boy who would leave you for this reason wouldn't have stayed long if you had given in. This type of boy is personally insecure and needs the reassurance of continual new conquests. If a date is only interested in your body, the sooner you find out, the better.

WHO SHOULD HOLD THE LINE?

Remember, popularity based on a reputation for petting is never satisfying, as you can never be sure you're really liked for yourself. Girls traditionally set the limits on how far to go; but since boys are aroused quicker and more easily, they should bear equal or greater responsibility in this area. As

Pat Boone warns, "Kissing for fun is like playing with a beautiful candle in a room full of dynamite."

TO THINK ABOUT

1. Pretend you are a parent, and make a list of the characteristics you would like to see in your child before you let him or her start dating.
2. Discuss the problems that might occur when a very young girl dates an older boy.
3. From observation or personal experience, review the advantages and disadvantages of going steady.
4. Comment on the difference between "necking" and "petting."
5. Is there anything wrong with petting "just a little" to be popular? How does the Bible rate "popularity" as a characteristic of a Christian?
6. Should you kiss on a first date?
7. Does a boy "earn" at least a little necking after an expensive date?
8. Discuss some inoffensive but effective ways of saying "no" to your date.
9. What if you really like a person, but every date with this boy or girl ends in a wrestling match?
10. List some specific situations which are most likely to lead to petting. Could Matthew 5:29 be applied to these situations?

DIGGING DEEPER

1. Run a private survey among your friends to see at what age most of them will or did start dating.
2. See if you can find out anything about dating customs in other countries.
3. Get three written (again unsigned) responses from boys who date in answer to the following question: "Would you like to date a pretty girl who is known for her 'heavy petting,' and why?"

CHAPTER 8

Dating Dangers

"Whether therefore ye eat,
or drink, or whatsoever ye
do, do all to the glory of
God."

1 Corinthians 10:31

Among the majority of the world's young people, dancing
is one of the mainstays when it comes to what to do on a
date. Many people also drink on dates, and some use drugs.
Obviously there are plenty of other things a person *could* do
on a date, such as the things discussed in chapter four. But
what if you *want* to dance—or drink—or try drugs?

Some people feel these things are fine, and others think
they are wrong. With such differences of opinion, it is lucky
we don't have to determine what is right and wrong solely
on the basis of what others think.

We have to be just as firm, however, about not deciding
what is right and wrong solely on the basis of what *we* think.
Obviously there is only one safe, unbiased authority of right
and wrong; and that is the Bible.

It might have been simpler if God had just given us a long
list of "Thou shalt's" and "Thou shalt not's." But God figured that if we grew spiritually, as He hoped, we wouldn't
need volumes of rules to cover every conceivable situation.

Instead, Christ taught in compact, ever-current principles, leaving the specific applications to us. So let's see
what guidelines the Bible offers on the topics of dancing,
drinking and drugs (Proverbs 18:13).

DANCING

It is difficult to view the subject of dancing objectively because not only is dancing fun, but it is often sanctioned and

sponsored by religious groups. The reasoning, "Everyone is doing it," more aptly fits this particular pastime than most of the others to which it is applied. Over 40 million Americans dance—can it really be wrong?

It would be terrible to condemn an activity which is actually perfectly all right. On the other hand, it would be terrible to condone an activity which is actually wrong. So let's really get down and examine the objections of those who don't feel Christians should dance.

DANCING IS SEXY

Each new style of dancing involves slightly different body movements. They are all basically sexual in appeal, however.

The pleasure of the old "slow" style of dancing was in the stimulating physical closeness of the partners swaying gently to romantic music. The excitement of current dance styles is in the sexy body movements, and no good dancer will deny this. Neither will any healthy boy deny that it is definitely sexually arousing to watch a girl swing her hips and breasts suggestively to music.

The Encyclopaedia Britannica states, "To a certain extent all dancing is sexually stimulating. . . ." And as a famous doctor recently said on TV, "It is ridiculous to say that one can dance in the modern fashion and not be sexually stimulated." So we have to admit that dancing is sexually stimulating—but does that make it wrong?

Let's read Jesus' words in Matthew 5:27-28 (Living New Testament).

> *"The laws of Moses said, 'You shall not commit adultery.' But I say: Anyone who even looks at a woman with lust in his eye has already committed adultery with her in his heart."*

Anything which causes us to have unwise sexual desires toward someone or which causes them to feel that way about us is wrong, and it has already been pointed out that dancing does stimulate sexual desire.

The word "unwise" is included because, as 1 Corinthians 7 points out, sexual desire between two who are married is fine. But that same desire toward one to whom you're not married is wrong. In other words, if your dancing is sexually exciting to you, your partner or anyone watching, Matthew 5:29 teaches you need to give it up.

IS IT CHRISTLIKE?

An old-fashioned argument against dancing which is particularly applicable to our modern style of dancing is God's condemnation of "lasciviousness" in such scriptures as Galatians 5:19-21. Greek dictionaries define the original word as "involving indecent bodily movements." A modern English dictionary says it means "something tending to produce lustful emotions." As pointed out before, dancing has to plead guilty on both counts. Such sensual emphasis is just not Christlike (1 Peter 4:1-4). Can you honestly imagine Christ twisting on a dance floor?

NO MAN IS AN ISLAND

Another point we can't avoid is that since dancing is considered a questionable activity by many Christians, a Christian who dances will definitely lose some of his favorable influence (Luke 17:1-2). Sometimes it is necessary to sacrifice personal pleasure in order to maintain a really good influence. Reading Romans 14:21-23 and 1 Corinthians 8:10-13 helps us realize and understand the important role "unselfishness" plays in the life of a Christian.

If a person decides not to dance, how does he go about explaining his position to others? Certainly not by bitterly condemning them or assuming a holier-than-thou attitude.

If he is invited to dance, he can tactfully decline. If asked why, he can gently but unapologetically explain his conviction that, as a Christian, dancing is not a part of God's will for his life (1 Peter 3:15). People are always more respected for saying "no" because of their convictions than for simply going along because of a lack of convictions.

DRINKING

Most states have laws making it illegal for anyone under 18 to have 3.2 beverages and allowing only those 21 or over to drink hard liquor. This solves the problem of drinking for

many teenagers, as a Christian is obligated to obey the laws
of the land (Titus 3:1). But moral convictions should go
much deeper than a law on paper.

Even with the more "sophisticated" option of drugs available now, drinking is still the number one drug abuse problem for teens. In the seventh through twelfth grade age
group, 28 percent are considered to be problem drinkers.

A majority of the people in our society drink, but it is
significant that one-third do not. In light of the many pressures encouraging drinking, these people apparently have
strong reasons for not doing so. Let's analyze some of the
facts.

EFFECTS OF ALCOHOL

Out of 55,000 highway deaths in the U.S. last year, 20,000
of them involved people who had been drinking. The F.B.I.
reports far more arrests related to drunkenness than any
other cause. A leading criminologist states that "the majority
of sex crimes are committed under the influence of alcohol."
Airlines do not allow their pilots to drink alcoholic beverages
within 24 hours of flying. These are all results of the fact that
alcohol diminishes clear thinking and self-control.

The dangers of drinking on a date are obvious. Scientists
affirm that alcohol lowers inhibitions and dulls the ability to
make keen judgments. God said so, too, in Isaiah 28:7.

Not only does alcohol greatly increase the likelihood of a
driving accident, but it makes young people too vulnerable
sexually, by dimming the inhibitions and convictions they
need in order to stay strong and morally pure. And these
dulling effects result not just from getting dead drunk, but
they begin with one can of beer or a single cocktail.

Drunkenness is specifically listed as a "work of the flesh"
in Galatians 5:21, and Paul writes that "they which do such
things shall not inherit the kingdom of God." The same
warning is repeated in 1 Corinthians 6:10. The Old Testament also made many references to the woes of the drunk-
ard (Psalms 107:27, Proverbs 20:1, Proverbs 23:20-21, 29-34,
Isaiah 19:14). But even most *non*religious people agree that it
is wrong to get drunk. The real question is over just a little
drinking—social drinking.

DAMAGES BRAIN

Everybody realizes that excessive drinking damages the brain, but recent studies show that even "moderate social drinking" destroys brain cells. In a report to the 28th International Congress on Alcohol and Alcoholism, Dr. Melvin Knisely showed evidence that when a drinker begins to feel giddy, some of his brain cells are being killed. He continued that "a heavy drinking bout can damage or destroy as many as 10,000 such cells."

Combine this with the fact that Dr. Denton Cooley, the famous heart transplant surgeon, says that brain transplants will never be possible because "cells of the brain and spinal cord, once destroyed never mend or grow back." Thus irreparable damage to our body is another important reason for the Christian not to drink (1 Corinthians 3:16-17).

ALCOHOL IS A NARCOTIC

Another problem is that alcohol is a habit-forming narcotic. Casual use tends to become habitual use.

Every alcoholic was at one time simply a light drinker who boasted he could "take it or leave it." It is true that only six out of every 100 social drinkers become alcoholics, but would you eat at a restaurant where "only six out of every 100" customers became critically ill?

The Institute of Scientific Studies for the Prevention of Alcoholism reports that out of every nine social drinkers, one will become a "problem drinker." No nondrinker ever became a problem drinker.

IF ANY MAN WILL COME AFTER ME

On this subject particularly, Paul's warning in Romans 14:21 comes to mind again. Paul specifically mentioned "drinking wine" as one of the things Christians must be willing to give up to avoid offending or weakening a brother. Problems such as drinking or dancing—and most other situations in life, as well—eventually come back to the need to make a choice between physical values and spiritual values. As Christ said in Matthew 16:24-26:

*If any man will come after me, let him deny himself,
and take up his cross, and follow me. For whosoever
will save his life shall lose it: and whosoever will lose
his life for my sake shall find it. For what is a man
profited, if he shall gain the whole world, and lose his
own soul?*

DRUGS

The subject of drugs is lengthy and complicated. Obviously there are some benefits to using them or people wouldn't do so. Each individual must analyze the pros and cons and then take an intelligent stand, based on conviction (1 Peter 3:15, Living New Testament).

COME FLY WITH ME

The promises of drugs are well-known. Depending on the type a person uses, they can induce him to "hear colors and see sounds," temporarily banish depression and boost energy, or simply "fly away from ones troubles for a while."

Drug pushers are eloquent about extolling the virtues. They have to be—they depend on selling to others to support their own habits. But what are the facts on the other side? Why do most people choose not to use drugs?

ARE HAPPINESS AND REALITY COMPATIBLE?

It is ironic that a generation so perceptive about cutting through the artificialities of life can then turn to the artificial—drugs—to seek peace and happiness. But happiness can only come when we face, and, if necessary, fix, reality. Anything which avoids reality is a deterrent to genuine happiness.

Drugs may offer a temporary escape, but a switch from one problem into another is no solution. Running away only leaves a person more exhausted and helpless. When the "high" wears off, the old problems are still there, compounded by a debilitating drug addiction. No war is ever won by continually running away from the conflict.

AT YOUR OWN RISK

Consider another reason to bypass drugs. All of the mind-altering drugs, including marijuana, induce changes in personality. Evidence is beginning to develop that this includes subtle permanent changes in the chemical processes of the brain cells.

From a purely selfish standpoint, are you willing to gamble with your mind and your own future? How about that of your future children?

Research data on the effects of drugs on unborn babies shows definite chromosomal changes. Embryo defects, such as missing limbs, appear in pregnant rats exposed to marijuana smoke.

Other effects of marijuana are a distortion of perception and reality. This results in impaired judgment, muscular incoordination, lagging attention span, poor memory recall and a faulty sense of time. Doctors estimate that one out of every 100 first-time marijuana users among college freshmen experiences "a serious panic episode . . . a bad trip . . . lasting a day or so."

Once you're into the drug culture, there is always the challenge to try something "bigger and better." Peer pressure will be great, and the cost high.

Recently a 29-year-old heroin addict died in jail while awaiting trial for burglary. He had reached the point where his habit required 75 bags daily at a cost of $750 a day. To get this kind of money, you either steal, prostitute or push drugs yourself—often all three.

ILLEGAL MEANS TROUBLE

Since drugs are illegal, they are sold through the black-market and at tremendous profits. The average heroin addict's habit costs him $60 a day—for an amount a drug company could produce for 40 cents.

Illegality also means a substance is not regulated by government agencies. Consequently, few drugs bought on the street are pure.

A person plays with death every time he buys a drug off the street. Marijuana has been found cut with manure and even Draino, the latter being fatal, of course.

If caught with drugs in your possession—you don't even have to be using them—you are charged with a felony. This could result in your permanently losing the right to vote, run for public office, own a gun, work for the city, county or federal government or get a job requiring bonding or licensing. This rules out ever becoming a doctor, teacher, realtor, lawyer, architect, stockbroker, beautician or engineer. Every job or credit application will carry information of your criminal record.

GET "HIGH" ON LIFE!

With all the beauty the world has to offer, the pleasures of an artificial "high" just aren't worth the risks. The next time someone asks if you "have the guts to turn on," ask them if they "have the guts *not* to."

Drugs allow their users to sidestep maturity and remain juvenile. The drug culture is an escape, a cop-out. And in a time when so much needs correction, it's going to take people who are clear-headed and strong to solve the problems.

Change will never occur by simply going off on some "trip." We need people who are high on life and not high on drugs, and Christian young people need to lead the way (1 Timothy 4:12)!

SUMMARY

The ability to perceive the difference between physical values and spiritual values is vital if one is to survive as a Christian. The battle between the flesh and the spirit is not just an interesting theological concept but a very real day-to-day conflict.

Read in Romans 7:14-15 of the agonizing struggle Paul had with this very problem. But Paul had found the answer, and that was Jesus Christ.

Just as love is called the very *heart* of Christianity, so the awareness of carnal versus spiritual could perhaps be referred to as the very *intellect* of Christianity. Paul summed it up in Romans 8:5-6:

> *"For they that are after the flesh do mind the things of the flesh; but they that are after the spirit the things of the spirit. For to be carnally minded is death; but to be spiritually minded is life and peace."*

CONSIDERATIONS

1. Show from the Bible that personal opinion is not a safe criterion for determining right and wrong.
2. See how "dancing" does on the 12 tests listed in chapter four.
3. What answer can you give to the old argument that 1 Timothy 5:23 condones drinking?
4. Now test "drinking" against the 12 questions in chapter four.
5. Comment on this reasoning: "I do it because it is no worse than . . . (some other evil)."
6. What do you personally consider to be the one strongest factor against using drugs?
7. Can you list ten things in this world that you think are beautiful enough on their own to not need the added stimulus of drugs?
8. What problem does marijuana's "judgment-impairing and inhibition-loosening" effect present to a Christian?
9. If a Christian considers the current narcotics laws to be unreasonable, is he justified in disregarding them? Why or why not?
10. Do you respect a person who engages in an activity which he believes is wrong?

DIGGING DEEPER

1. Each class member ask three boys who dance to write either "yes" or "no" on a folded piece of paper in answer to the following question: "Do you ever have sexual thoughts about the girl you're dancing with?" Collect all the papers and tabulate the results.
2. From the many Old Testament scriptures referring to strong drinks, compile a description of the man who drinks.
3. Do some library digging to find current statistics and the most recent results of medical research with marijuana and cocaine or whatever drugs are most popular with teens in your town.

Chapter 9

Why Wait?

"Avoid the passions of youth, and strive for righteousness, faith, love and peace, along with those who with a pure heart call for the Lord to help them."

2 Timothy 2:22
(Today's English Version)

"There are two sides to every question."

You've heard that comment many times. But on the subject of sex outside of marriage, there's only one side—the wrong side. God has said "No."

As Eve demonstrated, though, sometimes it is very hard for human beings to resist doing something they really want to do just because they've been told it's wrong. Perhaps that's why God said in Exodus 13 that parents must explain to their children, "This is done *because*. . . ."

Before examining the "whys" behind waiting, take a quick look at some of God's comments on this subject. What the world refers to as premarital sex or nonmonogamous marriage, God calls fornication; and He has the following to say about it:

Thou shalt not commit adultery (Exodus 20:14).

Whoever commits adultery with a woman lacks understanding; He who does so destroys his own soul. Wounds and dishonor he will get, and his reproach will not be wiped away (Proverbs 6:32, 33).

Now the works of the flesh are evident, which are: adultery, fornication, uncleanness, licentiousness. . . . those who practice such things will not inherit the kingdom of God (Galatians 5:19-21).

For this is the will of God, your sanctification: that you should abstain from sexual immorality . . . not in passion of lust, like the Gentiles who do not know God (1 Thessalonians 4:3-5).

Flee sexual immorality. Every sin that a man does is outside the body, but he who commits sexual immorality sins against his own body. Or do you not know that your body is the temple of the Holy Spirit who is in you, whom you have from God, and you are not your own? For you were bought at a price; therefore glorify God in your body (1 Corinthians 6:18-20).

It is obvious that God does not want His people to commit fornication. But underlying all of these verses is the plea that abstaining from sexual relations outside of marriage is for our own good.

Although it is possible to break any of God's laws—including those forbidding premarital sex—in disobedience it is more accurately *we* who are broken, rather than God's laws. Nothing demonstrates this more painfully than the problems which arise from sex outside of marriage.

PREGNANCY

The first problem which usually comes to mind is that of pregnancy, and this is certainly valid. Because of their high fertility, it is not uncommon for teens to become pregnant from having sexual relations only once.

Anyone who engages in intercourse risks becoming pregnant, even those using contraceptives. The only 100 percent safe contraceptive is abstinence. For those who become pregnant, the choices are giving birth and becoming a parent with all the incumbent responsibilities, giving the child up for adoption, or destroying that small life.

ABORTION

We often hear the fearful figures that one out of every four people will be stricken with cancer. But four times as many Americans were killed by abortion last year as were killed by cancer. More than 1.5 million girls resorted to abortion to destroy the unplanned life within them.

Few women come out of this traumatic, humiliating experience unscarred, if not physically then emotionally. Ending a life is not something one can easily forget.

The father doesn't get off easy either. He has to live forever with the remorse and guilt of the nightmare through which he put some girl—perhaps one he loved.

FORCED MARRIAGE

Of course, the other possibility is a hurried, hushed marriage—probably to the wrong person and at the wrong time. Ninety percent of the marriages forced by pregnancy end in divorce.

If a couple *has* to get married, it reveals a lack of responsibility that will become even more apparent in marriage. Such a marriage may result in many, many years of regret. God's plan is "one man, one wife, for life," even if the choice of partners was a poor one.

If the couple marries, they are often dismayed to find that sex is no longer as enjoyable for them. Besides the embittering fact that it was the reason they were forced to marry, some people find that once conditioned to the "forbidden fruit" aspect of illicit sex, they are unable to find sufficient excitement in married sex. It is foolish to risk a lifetime of enjoyment for a few months of stolen pleasure (Proverbs 9:17, 18).

VENEREAL DISEASE

Besides the danger of pregnancy, the possibility of venereal disease is another threat to those who engage in extramarital sex. Gonorrhea is the second most prevalent infectious disease in the United States, surpassed only by the common cold.

The sinister factor is that VD carriers look just like everyone else, except that they have within them a contagious sickness which can cause blindness, paralysis or insanity. The current epidemics of Herpes, AIDS and Chlamydea are but a few of the awful costs of violating God's "one man, one wife" rule. Fear is certainly not the *best* motivation but it is a valid one.

FALSE IMPRESSIONS

A girl's sexual responses are intimately linked with her feelings about the boy himself. A boy, however, can become excited sexually with much less emotional involvement. Naturally he responds to a girl he genuinely cares for. But he can also respond to a pretty face or figure.

A girl needs to realize that just because a boy tries to get intimate with her does not necessarily mean he loves her. Sex can masquerade as love for either of them and initiate some very unwise choices.

Often when a girl gives in and goes all the way with a boy, he takes her out once or twice again and then the relationship cools rapidly. Soon he drops her. It is unfair, but even boys who want to enjoy sex with their dates still usually want their prospective wives to be virgins.

REPUTATION

Another complication is that most of these boys talk too much. It is their insecurity which drives them to seek sexual "conquests" in the first place, and this same problem causes them to boast to others of their accomplishments. A good criteria has always been to live so that if the whole world knew what you did, you wouldn't have to be ashamed (Ecclesiastes 12:14).

GUILT

Even worse than the fear of others knowing about the sin is one's own guilt. The psalms cry out with the pain David continued to feel long after his sin of adultery with Bathsheba.

Guilt is never a simple burden to shake, and the guilt of fornication is particularly haunting. It will make a mockery of ones wedding vows, a deceit of the wedding night, and taunt parents trying to teach their children to be pure.

MARRIAGE PROBLEMS

Marriage, to the couple who has already had sexual relations, simply means additional responsibilities and restrictions—without the usual fresh discoveries and pleasures God planned. Add to the inexperience of premarital sex, the fear of being found out, and the inevitable guilt, and the results can only be less than ideal. This disappointment with initial sexual encounters can color attitudes toward the physical side of marriage for the rest of one's life.

Complete trust of each other's morality will never exist. Statistics show that couples who engaged in premarital sex have a far higher divorce rate than those who waited until marriage.

It is encouraging to know that, despite all the talk, "everybody" is *not* doing it. Even the flaunted Kinsey report found that 58 percent of male college freshmen had no sexual experience, and 80 percent of the 16- to 20-year-old unmarried women were still virgins.

When a girl is asked to give up her convictions, surrender her virtue, risk her reputation and take the chance of hurting herself and her family—does this really sound like love? Anyone who insists, "If you really loved me, you would!" can honestly be answered: "If you really loved me, you wouldn't!"

Many boys will attempt a few passes without actually expecting to get far. When girls tactfully refuse, most boys are not really hurt or angry but relieved. A boy often falls the hardest for the nice girl with whom he "can't get to first base."

Intimacy between a man and a woman is God's wedding gift to the newlyweds, and His gift is not to be opened early. "Love is patient . . ." (1 Corinthians 13:4).

TO THINK ABOUT

1. Whose responsibility is it to see that things don't get out of hand on a date?
2. List some specific things girls sometimes do which "lead boys on."
3. Is it possible to respond to someone physically without being in love with them?
4. How can premarital sex hinder satisfactory adjustment after marriage?
5. Why do you think boys often don't want to marry a girl with whom they're already having sexual relations?
6. Are there "extenuating circumstances," such as a couple

genuinely in love who will not be able to marry for several years?

7. Why are the odds all against a "forced marriage"?

8. If a couple is approaching the danger zone in this area, what are some specific things they can do to cool their dates a bit?

9. Is there any hope for the person who has already "gone too far"? (1 Corinthians 6:9-11)

10. How do you feel about a Christian and abortion?

DIGGING DEEPER

1. Read 1 Corinthians 6:16 and Ephesians 5:31. From these verses, do you see a fundamental reason why God forbids sexual relations outside of marriage?

2. Find out more about venereal disease, such as symptoms, effects, treatment, etc.

3. Several books have been written by girls about their feelings after an abortion. Find, read and review one of these.

CHAPTER 10

Am I Ready for Marriage?

"For which of you, intending to build a tower, sitteth not down first, and counteth the cost, whether he have sufficient to finish it?"

Luke 14:28

In Scheswig, Germany, a girl proves she is ready for marriage by being able to jump across a certain stream. In Nepal, a young girl must hike two miles uphill with a baby on her back to show she is ready to be a wife.

We consider such criteria rather humorous and totally illogical, but how *do* you determine whether you're ready for marriage? Immaturity is one of the leading causes of divorce, so perhaps a lot more thought should be given to this question.

EVERYBODY ELSE IS DOING IT

Too often when a couple's friends begin to marry and sexual pressures increase, the couple decides they will get married too. Other times marriage is seen as an escape from a childhood home which has become unpleasant. But neither of these reasons proves readiness for marriage any more than the test of jumping across a stream or hiking up a mountain.

AM I READY TO GIVE UP "ME"?

When a couple begins to seriously consider marriage, several questions should be given a lot of honest thought. One of these questions is: "Am I really ready to give up the carefree life of a single person?" (1 Corinthians 13:11)

Never again will you be able to think only of yourself and what you want (1 Corinthians 7:3-4). Are you ready to share all your possessions and all of your time?

Open communication is also vital to a sound relationship. Have you come to grips with yourself sufficiently to verbalize your feelings and desires to someone else? This is sometimes harder for boys than for girls. Are you willing to let down your facade and be the confidante and companion your partner will need?

The marital concept of becoming "one flesh" (Ephesians 5:31) involves more than just a sexual oneness. It involves a blending of hopes and fears, efforts and goals. Of course, with maturity comes the realization that it is this very lack of selfishness that is the secret of genuine happiness (Luke 17:33). But have you reached this point of maturity?

Someone has defined love as "the amount of selfish pleasure one person is willing to give up for another." Obviously, immaturity is not a characteristic belonging only to the young; but teenage marriages *are* three times more susceptible to failure, and marriage counselors attribute this high risk rate to immaturity.

In every day language, if you wanted to go to a movie and he or she was tired and would rather stay home, would you give up your desires graciously? Or would you act like a martyr, pouting and feeling mistreated?

If he enjoyed working on the car on Saturdays, would you find something else you could enjoy doing alone? If she wanted you to go shopping with her for a new dress, would you be willing to go along—even smile about it?

You should also ask yourself if you are physically ready for marriage. Biologically you have probably been ready for several years, and sex is one of the greatest incentives for marriage. In marriage you can enjoy sex without guilt or fear, which is never true outside of marriage (Hebrews 13:4).

If you have any qualms about this part of marriage, some competent counseling would be advisable. Occasionally children from overly cautious homes grow up with some unhealthy attitudes toward sex, and it will be much easier if you can get these out in the open and resolved before marriage.

HERE COMES THE STORK!

Along this line, it is also wise to consider whether you're ready to become a mother or father. You may think of that as years off yet, but babies have a way of arriving quite unscheduled sometimes. If you found yourself a prospective parent, are you ready—emotionally and financially?

DOLLARS AND SENSE

Many young people visualize in marriage the exquisite freedom they've been craving. Yes, when you're married you can eat pizza as often as you want—*if* you have enough money to buy it after paying the rent, electricity, car expenses, phone bill, furniture payment, insurance, water bill, taxes, doctor bills, etc. (Romans 13:8).

Money problems rate number one as a cause of marriage problems. Teenage husbands who work earn, on an average, less than $8,000 a year. Compare this with the salary of $20,000 plus that your father is probably making, and you'll begin to get a realistic picture of early marriage. The picture won't include new cars, dishwashers or fancy televisions and video recorders.

When you're first married, cramped quarters and hot dogs sound like fun. After all, you've got each other, and you're in love—what more could you ask? But fifteen years and several children from now, a comfortable house and money in the bank for emergencies will sound awfully good.

RING OR DIPLOMA—OR BOTH?

This brings up another question. Do you have enough education to secure a job with the potential to provide the things you'd like your family to have someday? Now you may feel perfectly willing to give up college for marriage, but the bitterness of having given up a desired career grows rather than fades through the years.

It is possible to be married and go to school at the same time, and many couples have fond memories of struggling to get through college during those early-married years. But if you decide to go that route, you need to realize a certain amount of thorns will accompany your bed of roses.

A wife's willingness to give up her education to work and put her husband through school is often more noble than wise. Those plans for the wife to get an education later after her husband has graduated get pushed further and further into the distance.

Too often childhood sweethearts marry, and the wife works hard to enable her husband to get his education. But then when the time comes for them to enjoy the fruit of their labors, he has entered another world intellectually; and they have nothing in common. Or babies have arrived.

Of course, one possibility is to live with (or off of) in-laws in the beginning; but God cautioned against this in Genesis 2:24 when He said that a couple were to *leave* their mother and father and cleave to each other. A boy should be able to support his wife himself if he is really ready for marriage (1 Timothy 5:8).

YOU WASH AND I'LL DRY

Marriage also means the taking on of many new responsibilities, not all of which are particularly romantic in nature. Do you find it tedious to keep your clothes washed and ready to wear and your room neat? With marriage, this chore will double!

Of course, it *is* more fun to clean and take care of your own house. But remember, there won't be a mother around to take over the dirty work like cleaning the bathroom and scrubbing the oven. Every button that gets sewed back on will be sewed on by you, and every dish that's washed will be washed by you.

The only food you'll have to eat will be what you cook, and that's a little frightening when you realize that 70% of today's brides don't know how to cook. It's been said that many modern young husbands can't tell if their wives are getting supper or defrosting the refrigerator.

Few budgets (and fewer stomachs) can survive a constant diet of TV dinners. So if you're weak in this area, grab a cookbook and hit the kitchen for a little "premarital experience." Your new husband will have enough adjustments to make without your learning to cook on him.

And boys, do you gripe about little jobs like mowing the

lawn or shoveling snow? When you accept the privileges of being a husband, you also will assume new responsibilities.

Financially, of course, you will be taking on a big responsibility; but also important are the small daily responsibilities. Little habits like leaving toothpaste on the sink or your dirty socks on the floor will not endear you to your wife.

Girls expect men to know how to fix things that break around the house and to help out with some of the big jobs. Matter of fact, most girls today expect their husbands to help them with such things as the cooking and cleaning—particularly if the wife is going to be working at an outside job.

It's wise to find out each other's philosophies in this area *before* marriage. Are you ready to take over your fair share of the responsibilities of running a house?

COUNTING THE COST

Marriage involves giving up much personal freedom, accepting some rules and restrictions and settling down to somewhat of a routine. In return, these responsibilities offer definite joys and securities. But you must decide which you prefer at this point in your life—a contented security or a little more time for being unencumbered and a bit irresponsible. Remember, once you marry there's no turning back (Mark 10:7-9).

As children, we first learned about love by being loved. We wanted and did what would make *us* happy. Later we learned to *like* others, but it was still basically because they made us happy.

Married love must progress far beyond this stage. Loving someone because they love you and make you happy is still basically selfish (Luke 6:33). Genuine love is caring enough about someone to do what will make *them* happy (1 Corinthians 7:33-34).

If you think you're in love, analyze it. Who is the greatest beneficiary of your love—you or the one you love? Marriage is great, but don't forget to count the costs as well as the benefits—and make sure you're willing to pay your share!

TO THINK ABOUT

1. What are some common but unwise reasons for getting married?
2. Would a girl benefit from a college education if she's planning to get married and be a housewife?
3. Discuss some characteristics of immaturity and show how they could be particularly harmful in a marriage.
4. Beside each of the following verses, list the responsibilities of a *wife* mentioned in that scripture.
   Genesis 2:18
   1 Timothy 5:14
   Titus 2:4, 5
   Proverbs 31:27, 28
   Ephesians 5:24, 33
5. After each of these verses, list the responsibilities of a *husband* described in that scripture.
   Ephesians 5:23, 33
   1 Peter 3:7
   Ephesians 6:4
   1 Timothy 5:8
   1 Corinthians 7:3, 4
6. Do you think the housework should be shared by husband and wife? Is there a Biblical basis for our traditional division of labor?
7. What problems can you imagine that could arise from being financially dependent on in-laws?
8. See what kind of budget you can set up for an income of $600 a month. Allow for *all* household expenses, such as a percentage of the annual car insurance, dental bills, etc.
9. Write down any advantages you think of which a person has who is not yet married.
10. Now list the advantages a married person has which a single person does not.

DIGGING DEEPER

1. For your own benefit, make a private list of the characteristics you feel you need to improve in before you get married.
2. See if you can find recent statistics relating age at time of marriage to marital success or failure.

3. Take an anonymous written survey among your married teenage friends as to the pros and cons and whether they would advise others to marry early.

CHAPTER 11

Is This the One?

"A worthy wife is her
husband's joy and crown;
the other kind corrodes his
strength and tears down
everything he does."

Proverbs 12:4
(The Living Bible,
Paraphrased)

Poor old Solomon, who had 700 wives (1 Kings 11:3), was certainly able to speak from experience when he wrote the above verse; and the statement is as true of a husband as it is of a wife. Except for the decision regarding your relationship to God, you will never make a more important decision than "Is this the one I should marry?"

The person you marry will probably be the outstanding influence affecting whether or not you live a faithful Christian life. This man or woman will determine whether your life is happy or miserable.

In no area is the old saying, "An ounce of prevention is worth a pound of cure" more true. If you make a mistake about whom you marry, there is no "cure" because God has decreed that marriage is for life (Romans 7:2).

WHAT YOU SEE IS WHAT YOU GET

People change very little after marriage, so it is extremely important to make sure that this is the person—just as he or she is—with whom you want to spend the rest of your life. To marry a person for just a few of his characteristics, planning to change the others you don't like, is foolish and unfair. It's been said that many girls would make better wives if they weren't so busy trying to make better husbands!

The difficulty lies in deciding which qualities are most important to you in a husband or wife. Obviously the person you marry will not be perfect. (If they were, they probably wouldn't marry *you*.) But it might be helpful to discuss a few of the fundamental areas marriage counselors have found to be important to a happy marriage (Amos 3:3).

THE FAMILY THAT PRAYS TOGETHER . . .

One of these basic areas of agreement should be a common faith. Facts show that the divorce rate for religiously-mixed marriages is two to three times higher than for homes where the husband and wife believe alike.

As discussed in detail in lesson three, religiously-mixed marriages which do not end in divorce must resolve serious personal, social, financial, in-law and child-rearing conflicts. Even more discouraging are the four out of seven odds that the Christian partner in such a relationship will eventually lose his own faith (Deuteronomy 7:3-4).

In a recent Bible class, a friend was discussing the problems of putting Christ first (Matthew 6:33) when married to an unbeliever. Although she still loved her husband, her concluding advice to anyone considering marrying out of the church was "Don't"!

With tears in his eyes, the leader of the group agreed. "When I first married," he said, "I felt sure my wife would become a Christian within six months. But that was 22 years ago, and my hope for her grows less each day."

If you are in love with someone who is not a Christian, the answer is not to just give them up. Instead, make your own life so beautifully overflowing with the joys of Christianity that the one you love cannot possibly resist accepting the Christian way of life also (Matthew 5:16).

What better way is there to really show your love for someone! Then you not only will have won a better husband or wife for yourself but will have given the one you love the gift of eternal life and heaven (James 5:20).

But do this *before* you marry! Then you will find out in time if they are wise enough (Proverbs 1:7) and sufficiently tender-hearted to be moved by the love of God. If not, summon all your courage and spiritual strength and end the relationship (2 Corinthians 6:14). It will hurt terribly for awhile, but you'll be rewarded some day when you experience the joy of serving God side by side with one you love.

IS THIS A SOUND BUSINESS VENTURE?

Similar economic and educational backgrounds are also helpful to a happy marriage. God has said that the husband is to be the head of the family (Ephesians 5:23) and his wife is to respect and submit to him (Ephesians 5:24, 33). You can see the problems which will arise in following this command if a girl is economically or educationally superior to her husband.

After the honeymoon, marriage soon settles down to a very practical and human relationship. In one sense, marriage is like a newly-formed business partnership.

It is important that the two involved have similar feelings about money and its use. A boy reared in a very thrifty family in which money was always tight will often disagree with the economic attitudes of a girl from a financially comfortable family in which luxuries and whims were usually indulged.

More basically, an easy-going individual content to work just enough to eat and own the bare essentials would be very wise to avoid marrying an ambitious person with expensive tastes (Proverbs 15:27). It is also important to agree on *how* you will earn your money. A boy who plans to farm, for example, had better be sure his financee wants to be a farmer's wife.

A successful doctor's wife will have to be self-sufficient and adaptable, as her husband, and their time together, will never be completely her own. And if a wife is planning to continue her career, her husband should know ahead of time and be willing to encourage her and accept any consequent inconveniences good-naturedly.

IN-LAWS OR OUT-LAWS

Another way of determining whether a person is right for you is to spend some time with his family. Would you be satisfied if your boyfriend turned out to be like his father or your girlfriend like her mother? They probably will, you know.

It's frustrating, but no matter how annoyed a person is with his parents' "mistakes," studies show that he will probably make the same ones when he gets married. A girl whose mother nagged a lot is very likely to nag her own husband.

Compare the way your family lives with the way his family likes to do things. If your family makes a big occasion out of birthdays and Christmas, while your date's family shuns sentimentality and considers one day the same as the next, conflicts may be in store. Ideal closeness is difficult if one partner comes from a family with little conversation except concerning the daily necessities, while in the other family a discussion is always going on about something, whether it's who lost the car keys or our country's foreign policy.

What basic roles do the men and women in the family play? Do the men spend their evenings around the TV while the women putter in the kitchen? Remember, your mate learned what his role in life is to be from his parents and their examples. We're all, to some extent, products of our environment; so beware if you find his "environment" too strange.

While you're there, see if you can sneak a peek at your date's room. It will probably reveal a lot about his basic personal habits. (Frightening thought, isn't it!) But after marriage when the urgencies of sexual attraction begin to level off, these are the day-to-day type things that will either draw you closer or drive you crazy.

TWENTY QUESTIONS

While you're dating, talk over everything you can think of, but especially areas about which you feel strongly. Don't just assume that he or she feels the same as you. Occasionally people are married happily several years and then heartbroken to discover a fact that should have been discussed before marriage, such as their mate's preference not to have children.

THE MATCH GAME

Consider also your emotional needs. A person who is very warm-natured and affectionate will suffer a lot of unhappiness if married to a cool, remote, self-contained individual.

Some people require a continual sharing and thrive on total togetherness and lots of conversation, while others are basically loners, preferring to keep most of their thoughts to themself. Whichever you are, you would be wise to find a mate of similar temperament. If one partner craves more intimacy than the other feels the need of giving, both will be miserable a great deal of the time!

IT'S WHAT'S INSIDE THAT COUNTS

It might be helpful to actually list the personal qualities you admire in people, such as patience, dependability, a sense of humor, thoughtfulness, good manners, kindness, etc. Then see how many of these traits are characteristic of your boyfriend or girlfriend.

If they fall very short of your ideal, do both of you a favor and delay the wedding awhile. It is so very important to realize that these basic inner qualities are what will make that person a good husband or wife!

Five years after you're married, how tall he is or how terrific a figure she has will seem relatively unimportant (1 Samuel 16:7). Make sure the characteristics you admire in your girlfriend or boyfriend are ones that will last and still be important several years from now.

A survey of newlyweds conducted by a national magazine summarized the following qualities that had attracted them to their mates: "Sex appeal, looks, popularity, social ease and impression on others."

Ten years later, the partners were questioned again. Their new lists completely omitted "looks" and "popularity" and read like this: "Ability to communicate freely, mutual desire for the other's company, sensitivity, sexual attraction and a feeling of family responsibility." So analyze carefully what appeals to you about this person.

ASK YOURSELF

Would this person be good to grow old with? Is he or she thoughtful and considerate of my wishes? Does he get along well with others, and is he willing to compromise when we disagree?

Is he a man I will gladly "respect and obey" (Colossians 3:18)? Can I love and honor this girl as myself (Ephesians 5:28)? Will this individual make a good father or mother for my future children? Do they challenge and inspire the very best in me—spiritually, mentally, physically and emotionally?

Most premarital counselors feel six months of regular dating is the minimum time in which you could get to know a person well enough to evaluate him or her as a marriage partner. Too often couples confuse sexual attraction for love and never really get to know each other until after marriage.

Remember, this is a lifetime partnership you're considering forming. "Til death do us part" now means about 50 years! So if you're not sure, wait.

CONSIDERATIONS

1. It has been said that "Love Conquers All." Do you agree with this statement and explain why.
2. Is it possible to have a happy life despite an unhappy marriage? Give your reasons.
3. What traits do you think a young teenager might look for in a date which would be relatively insignificant in a husband or wife?
4. Why does strong sexual attraction sometimes get in the way of making a valid analysis of a person as a potential marriage partner?
5. In what specific ways could the person you marry affect how faithfully you live the Christian life?
6. In what ways should the Christian life be far superior to any other way of life and thus appeal to a future mate?
7. Write down some basic questions it would be important for a man and woman to discuss before marriage.
8. Does the Bible have anything to say about homosexual relationships?
9. Can you think of ways other than those already mentioned of determining if a person is right for you to marry?

10. Read Matthew 7:7, 11 and John 15:7. Then discuss whether it is appropriate to pray for God to send you a good husband or wife.

DIGGING DEEPER

1. Each class member ask someone who has been married 10 years or more to write down what they consider to be the five most important qualities for a husband or wife to have. (Girls should ask wives and boys husbands and the results compiled separately.)
2. Make and save a list of the characteristics you personally think are important for the person you'll marry to have. (Later when you think you've found that person, compare him or her to your list.)
3. Now make a list of characteristics you particularly dislike in people, saving this list also to some day check out your potential husband or wife.

CHAPTER 12

What God Hath Joined

". . . For this cause shall a man leave father and mother, and shall cleave to his wife: and they twain shall be one flesh. Wherefore they are no more twain, but one flesh. What therefore God hath joined together, let not man put asunder."

Matthew 19:5, 6

Although all brides are beautiful and all grooms handsome and charming, the fairy tale beginning doesn't always last. Statistics show that marriage is one of the riskiest ventures you can enter.

One out of every nine people in the United States is divorced. Anywhere from one fourth to one third of all marriages end in divorce, and the figure rises to forty percent if you include annulments and desertions.

What causes a beautiful, idealistic love to turn into bitter hatred? According to counselors who specialize in marriage problems, the two leading problems are:

1. A lack of commitment to the marriage
2. Inability to accept responsibility

Breaking these two generalizations down into specifics, the main areas of disagreement leading to divorce are as follows: sex, money, children, alcohol, in-laws, religion (interfaith marriages) and gambling.

LACK OF COMMITMENT

The first of the two major problems listed as contributing to divorce is a lack of commitment. The Christian couple has a real advantage in this area, as they know they *have* to make the marriage. God has ruled out divorce (Luke 16:18). Probably that is one reason God gave this law—so a man and woman would go into marriage with the commitment necessary to make it happy and successful.

Let's lay the groundwork for this particular study by reading a few of the Bible verses that apply:

"It hath been said, 'Whosoever shall put away his wife, let him give her a writing of divorcement:' But I say unto you, That whosoever shall put away his wife, saving for the cause of fornication, causeth her to commit adultery: and whosoever shall marry her that is divorced committeth adultery."

Matthew 5:31, 32

"Whosoever putteth away his wife, and marrieth another, committeth adultery: and whosoever marrieth her that is put away from her husband committeth adultery."

Luke 16:18

"For the woman which hath an husband is bound by the law to her husband so long as he liveth; but if the husband be dead, she is loosed from the law of her husband. So then if, while her husband liveth, she be married to another man, she shall be called an adulteress: but if her husband be dead, she is free from that law; so that she is no adulteress, though she be married to another man."

Romans 7:2, 3

"And unto the married I command, yet not I, but the Lord, Let not the wife depart from her husband: But and if she depart, let her remain unmarried, or be reconciled to her husband: and let not the husband put away his wife."

1 Corinthians 7:10, 11

IS THE GRASS REALLY GREENER?

Was God being narrow-minded and unreasonable to write such a strict law? A little thought will reveal that it was not harshness but understanding that formed the rule.

After you marry, you will become very provoked with your husband or wife sometimes, perhaps even to the point of thinking maybe you made a mistake in marrying them. The simple truth is that no matter who you marry, he or she will have faults—some of which will annoy you immensely. This is true of the most ideal-appearing husband and wife you know.

You may find indirect comfort in the fact that people who divorce and remarry have an even higher divorce rate than first-time marriages. God knew that happiness in marriage didn't depend nearly as much on the one you marry as on your own attitudes. Thus we begin to see the reasoning in His telling us to stick it out with the first person we marry.

Assuming you used fairly good sense in picking your mate in the first place, you wouldn't really be any better off if you were to try again. Human nature always suspects that "the grass is greener on the other side of the fence." So if God hadn't simplified things for us by saying we *had* to stay with our first husband or wife, people would probably spend most of their lives marrying and remarrying, always hoping to improve on the last marriage.

IT TAKES A MOMMY AND A DADDY

Perhaps God was also thinking of children when He said divorce is wrong. A child from a broken home is six times more likely to become delinquent, and the odds of his marriage ending in divorce are much higher than normal.

Children need the love and guidance of two parents (Proverbs 1:8). To rob them of this is to destroy part of their birthright and jeopardize their future happiness.

IF ONE PARTNER IS UNFAITHFUL

God has made one exception to his "Marriage is for Life" rule, and that is in the case of adultery. A couple who sleeps together becomes one (1 Corinthians 6:16). Thus a person who has intercourse with someone other than their legal mate is in one sense forming a new union, and God says the old one can be ended (Matthew 5:32).

This in no sense absolves the one who committed adultery. 1 Corinthians 6:9-10 and Galatians 5:19-21 specifically list "adultery" as one of the sins which can keep people out of heaven. But it does free the innocent partner from the unfaithful one, and the freed partner can remarry without committing sin (Matthew 5:31, 32).

Adultery is a "symptom" of marriage problems, however, and seldom a "cause." In fact, adultery ranks way down in seventeenth place among reasons given for divorce.

DIVORCE NO CURE-ALL

Even when allowed by God, divorce is exceedingly painful. It is the separation of two who were one flesh; (Matthew 19:5-6); and, like any surgery, it is painful.

For a woman, there are very few unmarried men of her age left. So she has to resign herself to probably working and living alone for the rest of her life. Seven million women in the United States head households and work to support themselves.

Men don't escape either. If the couple has children, they will probably be taken from him. And a married man doesn't know what scrimping is until he tries getting a divorce and remarrying and then having to support *two* families. Alimony cuts a man's living standards just about in half.

WARTS AND ALL!

The real solution is, as Billy Graham puts it, simply accepting your mate—warts and all! Learn to *like* him as well as love him.

Wipe out of your mind all the "What if's" and "if only's" (Luke 9:62), and follow Paul's advice in Philippians 4:8 to think on his virtues. This is the old, familiar "Think Positive" approach to life; but it works, and especially well in marriage.

ADVICE FROM A BACHELOR

Paul gave some more good marital advice in 1 Corinthians 13:5 when he wrote that "Love seeketh not her own, is not easily provoked." Think how many quarrels would have been avoided if somebody had not gotten provoked!

A sense of humor is one of the very best "ounces of prevention" for marriage problems. When he complains that the meat is a bit tough, she can either respond with a laugh and "But it lasts longer that way!" (Proverbs 15:1, 16:32)—or with a glare and "If you don't like it, cook it yourself!" (James 3:5). The type of response the wife chooses (Proverbs 18:21) will make quite a difference in the way the rest of the evening goes, as well as the way the rest of the marriage goes.

THIS IS YOUR LIFE—AND EVERYONE ELSE'S

Other complaints often heard by divorce counselors are:
"He never talks to me."
"She cares more about what others think than how I feel."
"He doesn't appreciate me."
"She isn't interested in anything I do."
"He's always criticizing me in public."

When problems arise in your marriage—and they will occasionally—remember that what you are experiencing is simply normal marriage, no different from anyone else's. You just don't see other people's problems as clearly, because most of us have developed highly-illusive facades for our public images.

No really worthwhile accomplishment ever comes without effort, and a happy marriage is definitely a worthwhile accomplishment. Just remember, the attitude that marriage is for keeps will do more than anything else to make your marriage the "Happily Ever After" kind.

CONSIDERATIONS

1. For what reasons were divorces granted in the Old Testament?
2. The wedding vows say, "For better or for worse, for richer or for poorer." What if your mate turns out to be mainly "worse" and "poorer"?
3. Is it possible to "love" a person without "liking" them?
4. Is the "annulment" of a marriage scriptural?

5. Could the old adage, "There are two sides to every question" be true when a marriage breaks up because one partner committed adultery? How?
6. Is it essential to get a divorce when one partner has been unfaithful?
7. In what ways do children suffer from a divorce?
8. When differences are "irreconcilable," can two people scripturally separate as long as they don't remarry?
9. What does the Bible say about a divorced person re-marrying, and could you scripturally marry a divorced person?
10. List the places in or near your community to which a couple having marriage problems could go for help.

DIGGING DEEPER

1. Find out how many marriages and divorces there were in your city last year and what your local divorce rate is. Also see if you can find out how many children were in-volved.
2. Ask someone in a counseling position, such as a doctor, minister, judge or social worker, to list what they feel are the five most common reasons for divorce. Even better, arrange for them to spend some time talking to the class.
3. Tactfully ask any divorced people you know if they would mind writing down for you the hardest things about di-vorce.

CHAPTER 13

Happily Ever After . . .

"Live happily with the
woman you love through
the fleeting days of life, for
the wife God gives you is
your best reward down here
for all your earthly toil."
> Ecclesiastes 9:9
> (The Living Bible,
> Paraphrased)

At last the showers and the wedding and the rice-throwing are all finished, and the "happily ever after" part can begin. You can finally sign your names as "Mr. and Mrs."

But marriage is not an agreement between just a man and a woman. It is a three-way agreement between you, your mate and God. This concept of God as an active partner in your marriage is very basic to its success.

"Except the Lord build the house, they labour in vain that build it. . . ."

> *Psalms 127:1*

I TOOK OUT THE GARBAGE YESTERDAY

Traditional marriage "roles" have changed quite a bit in the last few years. Now many husbands can be found in the kitchen preparing gourmet meals while the wives are out earning hefty paychecks. Yet these are just superficial changes.

A husband is still to be the head of his wife (Ephesians 5:23), he is to support her (1 Timothy 5:8) and to love her as his own body (Ephesians 5:28). A wife is still to obey her husband (1 Peter 3:1), respect him (Ephesians 5:33) and be his helper (Genesis 2:18, 1 Corinthians 11:9).

These responsibilities do not make one *superior* to the other, but they do make each *different* from the other. If these basic differences are observed, they will solve a lot of problems and insure happiness. The unhappy marriages you see are a direct result of someone disregarding the rules and inherent differences God built into marriage.

THE BEST MARRIAGE MANUAL

If you'd like to read a good book on how to have a successful marriage, let me recommend the Bible! Look at Proverbs 15:17, for example, which says, "Better is a dinner of herbs where love is, than a stalled ox and hatred therewith."

In modern language that translates, "Better is a peanut butter sandwich with a calm and happy mother than veal scallopini served by a harried, fussy mother." I'll bet you'd agree that's good advice!

Here is another excerpt from God's marriage manual:

> *". . . you married women should adapt yourselves to your husbands. . . . Your beauty should not be dependent on an elaborate coiffure, or on the wearing of jewelry or fine clothes, but on the inner personality— the unfading loveliness of a calm and gentle spirit. . . . Similarly, you husbands should try to understand the wives you live with, honoring them as physically weaker yet equally heirs with you of the grace of eternal life. . . . To sum up, you should all be of one mind living like brothers with true love and sympathy for one another, generous and courteous at all times. Never pay back a bad turn with a bad turn or an insult with another insult, but on the contrary pay back with good."*
>
> *(1 Peter 3:1-9, Phillips paraphrase).*

One of the most beneficial insights you could gain from this entire study is that the Bible is truly relevant to our everyday needs. Proverbs 14:1 warns that the "wise woman *buildeth* her house; but the foolish plucketh it down with her hands." In paraphrased form below is more advice taken from the Bible on how to build a happy home.

Put God first in your family.

(Matthew 6:33)

Don't let a job and money become too important.
                                              (Proverbs 15:27)

Comfort and encourage your partner when he or she is discouraged.

                                              (Ecclesiastes 4:9-10)

Be generous with compliments.
                                              (Proverbs 3:27)

Concentrate on each other's good points.
                                              (Philippians 4:8)

Think before you blurt.
                                              (Proverbs 15:28)

Don't feel compelled to say everything you think!
                                              (Proverbs 29:11)

Overlook slights and offenses; be slow to anger.
                                              (Proverbs 19:11)

A gentle response will head off a lot of arguments.
                                              (Proverbs 15:1)

Do nothing out of pride or strife.
                                              (Philippians 2:3)

Hear your mate out before you present your side.
                                              (Proverbs 18:13)

Admit it when you're wrong, and pray about major differences.

                                              (James 5:16)

Never go to sleep angry with one another.
                                              (Ephesians 4:26)

Be more concerned with giving than getting.
                                              (Acts 20:35)

Put the other's wishes and feelings before your own.
                                              (Philippians 2:4)

Be as courteous to each other as you are to strangers.
                                              (1 Peter 3:8)

Find out your mate's feelings before making major deci-
sions.

(*Psalms 54:14*)

Keep confidences confidential—even from best friends.

(*Proverbs 25:19*)

Try to understand each other's idiosyncrasies.

(*Proverbs 20:5*)

A tiny apartment with peace of mind beats a luxurious
house with problems.

(*Proverbs 21:9*)

Save a little extra to see you through emergencies.

(*Proverbs 10:5*)

Learn to be content regardless of external circum-
stances.

(*Philippians 4:11*)

Don't be stingy with each other sexually.

(*1 Corinthians 7:4*)

Be affectionate—no problem now, but remember in 10
years.

(*Romans 12:10*)

Nothing improves a relationship like a happy disposi-
tion.

(*Proverbs 17:22*)

Pray for your marriage!

(*Matthew 18:19*)

PASS THE KETCHUP

Any boarding house can provide three meals a day and a
place to sleep, but a home feeds the heart. Marriage is the
most intimate and satisfying of human relationships; it is
love at its highest earthly level. But marriage is also learning
30 different ways to cook hamburger meat and making $1.83
stretch until payday.

Marriage is picking out your first Christmas tree together.

It's finding just the right spot for each wedding gift and opening a joint checking account.

Marriage is finding out that he hates scrambled eggs and that she loves ketchup on hers. It's discovering that he yodels in the shower and she uses scotch tape to curl her hair.

It's thinking maybe you're pregnant and being worried and hopeful at the same time. It's the simple pleasure of going to a movie and then coming back to your own home together rather than to your separate houses like before. It's also the bleak depression of your first big fight and the maturity that comes with working it out.

LOVE IS NOTHING 'TIL YOU GIVE IT AWAY

In marriage, you will enjoy your mate most of the time and learn to endure him the rest of the time. But under it all you will know there is love, and every human being needs this love.

With love, though, the more you give, the more you get. So give freely!

TO THINK ABOUT

1. Titus 2:4-5 instructs older women to teach the younger to "love their husbands." Can "love" be "learned?"
2. What is involved in a man's being "head of the house" (Ephesians 5:23)? How does this fit with the instruction in 1 Timothy 5:14 that women are to "guide the house?"
3. What are the implications of a man loving his wife "as much as he loves himself" (Ephesians 5:33)? How will this show?
4. Does the husband have any responsibility in regard to submission? Read Galatians 5:13 and Ephesians 5:21.
5. In what specific ways can a woman be a "helpmeet" (Genesis 2:18) for her husband?
6. List the accomplishments of the ideal wife as described in Proverbs 31, and suggest modern-day counterparts.
7. Is it possible for a woman to be happy if she must care for the needs of her husband? Tie in with Matthew 20:25-28.

8. All marriages have quarrels. Discuss some guidelines for "fighting fairly."
9. What qualifications of an elder or deacon relate to his marriage (Titus 1:5-9, 1 Timothy 3:1-13)?
10. Discuss how the quality of one's marriage affects the quality of his spirituality (1 Peter 3:7, Matthew 5:23-24).

DIGGING DEEPER

1. Many lists have been compiled of "formulas" for a happy marriage. See if you can find one, and read it in class.
2. From your own observations of married people, write some rules you think would be helpful to a marriage.
3. After studying the many scripture references in the past 13 lessons, can you think of any helpful principles of life which the Bible does not either directly or indirectly teach us?

NOTES